PELICAN BOOKS

THE EUROPEAN WITCH-CRAZE
OF THE 16TH AND 17TH CENTURIES

Hugh Redwald Trevor-Roper, the son of a doctor, was born in
1914 at Glanton, Northumberland. He was educated at Charter
House and Christ Church, Oxford, where he read Classics, in
which he was awarded several distinctions, and Modern History.
From 1937 to 1939 he was Research Fellow of Merton College.
During the war he held a commission in Military Intelligence,
and was engaged on work of a secret nature. After the war he
returned to Oxford as a Student of Christ Church, and in 1957
was appointed Regius Professor of Modern History. He published
his first book, *Archbishop Laud*, in 1940; in 1947 he published
The Last Days of Hitler, an immediate best-seller which has
been translated into sixteen languages. In 1957 his *Historical
Essays* were published, and in 1964 he edited a series of essays
collected in honour of Sir Keith Feiling on his eightieth birth-
day. His more recent publications include *Religion, Reformation
and Social Change* (1967); *The Rise of Christian Europe* (1965);
The Age of Expansion (1968); *The Philby Affair* (1968). Professor
Trevor-Roper married Lady Alexandra Howard-Johnston, daughter of the late Field-Marshal Earl Haig, in 1954. His chief interests are literature, country life, and field sports.

The European Witch-Craze of the 16th and 17th Centuries

———————————*———————————

H. R. TREVOR-ROPER

> A commonly received error is never utterly
> overthrown, till such time as we go from
> signs unto causes, and shew some manifest
> root or fountain thereof common unto all,
> whereby it may clearly appear how it hath
> come to pass that so many have been over-
> seen. – RICHARD HOOKER, *Of the Laws of
> Ecclesiastical Polity*, I, viii, 3

PENGUIN BOOKS

Penguin Books Ltd, Harmondsworth, Middlesex, England
Penguin Books Australia Ltd, Ringwood, Victoria, Australia

—

This study first published in the collection of the author's essays,
Religion, the Reformation and Social Change, by Macmillan & Co. Ltd
First published separately, in slightly revised form, in Pelican Books 1969
Copyright © H. R. Trevor-Roper, 1967, 1969

—

Made and printed in Great Britain
by Hazell Watson & Viney Ltd
Aylesbury, Bucks
Set in Linotype Granjon

CONTENTS

FOREWORD TO THE PELICAN EDITION

THIS study of the European witch-craze was originally written to complete a series of essays which were published together in 1967 under the title *Religion, the Reformation and Social Change*. All those essays were concerned, in one way or another, with what I called, in one of them, 'the General Crisis of the seventeenth century': a crisis which, I suggested, was not merely political – though it led to political revolution in many countries – but arose out of deep tensions in the very structure of society. This essay on 'the General Crisis', when first published in *Past and Present*, led to an animated discussion, in the course of which the distinguished French historian, M. Roland Mousnier, went even further than I had gone. The sixteenth and seventeenth centuries in Europe, he suggested, saw not only a general social crisis but 'an intellectual mutation'; and he referred particularly to the end of Aristoteleanism and the growth of belief in witchcraft as 'aspects which would need to be studied if we really want to talk of the crisis of the seventeenth century'. When I read these words by M. Mousnier, I recognized their force, and I decided to follow his advice and make a profounder study of the rise and decline of the witch-craze in the sixteenth and seventeenth centuries, and to see it, if possible, not in isolation, as a mere aberration of the human mind, but in its context, as a phenomenon of human society.

I know that some critics may object. They may say that the witch-craze is a disgusting subject, below the dignity of history. To them I would reply that, disgusting or not, it is also a historical fact, of European significance, and its rise precisely in the years of the Renaissance and Reformation is a problem which must be faced by anyone who is tempted to over-emphasize the 'modernity' of that period. Ugly though it may be, we can no more overlook it, in our attempts to understand the 'early modern' period of our history, than we can overlook the equally ugly phenomenon of antisemitism in 'contemporary' history. I therefore set out to look at the craze as a whole, throughout Europe, and, if possible, to relate its rise, frequency and decline to the general intellectual and social movements of the time, from which I believe that any such movement is inseparable.

The result of my study surprised me. When I began it I was influenced by M. Mousnier's remark, which implied – or seemed to me to imply – that the rise of the witch-craze coincided with the decline of Aristoteleanism, and that there was a causal connexion between that rise and this decline. This view coincided with that of the late Lucien Fèbvre, who saw the witch-craze as being in some way fostered by the spread of Renaissance Platonism and the Platonic belief in 'demons'. But my own studies led me to a very different conclusion. It will be seen that, to me, the growth of belief in witchcraft is a by-product, in specific social circumstances, of that hardening and extension of Aristoteleanism (or rather, of the pseudo-Aristoteleanism of the Schoolmen) which had begun in the later Middle Ages and was intensified both by Catholics and Protestants after the Reformation. It is not a new force, generated by the decomposition of an old cosmology. It is the underside of that cosmology, a social rationalization, which went down, with it, in the general social and intellectual revolution of the mid seventeenth century. And Renaissance Platonism, for all its demons – which were ultimately demonizations of natural forces, not diabolical saboteurs of them – was an agent not of its expansion but of its dissolution.

One further point evidently needs to be made, or rather repeated. In this essay I am not concerned with mere witch-beliefs: with those elementary village credulities which anthropologists discover in all times and at all places. How those beliefs are motivated and how they should be interpreted is a problem which may legitimately be studied. But it is not my problem, and those critics who have censured me for not entering more sympathetically into the mental processes of the peasantry are barking up the wrong tree. They cannot claim that I have misdirected them, for I have always made my position in the other tree perfectly clear. They have only to look at the third paragraph of my essay. However, for their benefit I repeat it. My subject is not witch-beliefs, which are universal, but the witch-craze, which is limited in space and in time; and by the 'witch-craze' I mean the inflammation of those beliefs, the incorporation of them, by educated men, into a bizarre but coherent intellectual system which, at certain socially determined times, gave to otherwise unorganized peasant credulity a centrally directed, officially blessed persecuting force. The 'witch-craze' as I have defined it is as different from mere witch-beliefs as the mythology concerning the Elders of Zion is from the mere dislike of Jews – which also, no doubt, can be sympathetically studied by those who believe that every illusion, provided it is entertained by the lower classes, is innocent and worthy of respect.

For this Pelican edition of my essay I have made a few small additions and adjustments. I am grateful to those friends and correspondents who have sometimes spotted an error or a solecism to be corrected.

Oxford   H. R. TREVOR-ROPER
21 November 1967

I

THE NEW DIABOLICAL RELIGION

THE European witch-craze of the sixteenth and seventeenth centuries is a perplexing phenomenon : a standing warning to those who would simplify the stages of human progress. Ever since the eighteenth century we have tended to see European history, from the Renaissance onwards, as the history of progress, and that progress has seemed to be constant. There may have been local variations, local obstacles, occasional setbacks, but the general pattern is one of persistent advance. The light continually, if irregularly, gains at the expense of darkness. Renaissance, Reformation, Scientific Revolution mark the stages of our emancipation from medieval restraints. This is natural enough. When we look back through history we naturally see first those men, those ideas, that point forward to us. But when we look deeper, how much more complex the pattern seems! Neither the Renaissance nor the Reformation nor the Scientific Revolution are, in our terms, purely or necessarily progressive. Each has a Janus-face. Each is compounded both of light and of darkness. The Renaissance was a revival not only of pagan letters but of pagan mystery-religion. The Reformation was a return not only to the unforgettable century of the Apostles but also to the unedifying centuries of the Hebrew kings. The Scientific Revolution was shot through with Pythagorean mysticism and cosmological fantasy. And beneath the surface of an ever more sophisticated society what dark passions and inflammable credulities do we find, sometimes accidentally released, sometimes deliberately mobilized! The belief in witches is one such force. In the sixteenth and seventeenth centuries it was not, as the prophets of progress might suppose, a lingering ancient superstition, only waiting to dissolve. It was a new explosive force, constantly and fearfully expanding with the passage of time. In those years of apparent illumination there was at least one quarter of the sky in which darkness was positively gaining at the expense of light.

Yes, gaining. Whatever allowance we may make for the mere multiplication of the evidence after the discovery of the art of printing, there can be no doubt that the witch-craze grew, and grew terribly, after the Renaissance. Credulity in high places increased, its engines of expression were made more terrible, more victims were sacrificed to it. The years 1550–1600 were worse than the years 1500–1550, and the years 1600–1650 were worse still. Nor was the craze entirely separable from the intellectual and spiritual life of those years. It was forwarded by the cultivated popes of the Renaissance, by the great Protestant reformers, by the saints of the Counter-Reformation, by the scholars, lawyers and churchmen of the age of Scaliger and Lipsius, Bacon and Grotius, Bérulle and Pascal. If those two centuries were an age of light, we have to admit that, in one respect at least, the Dark Age was more civilized.

For in the Dark Age there was at least no witch-craze. There were witch-beliefs, of course – a scattered folk-lore of peasant superstitions: the casting of spells, the making of storms, converse with spirits, sympathetic magic. Such beliefs are universal, in time and place, and in this essay I am not concerned with them. I am concerned with the organized, systematic 'demonology' which the medieval Church constructed out of those beliefs and which, in the sixteenth and seventeenth centuries, acquired a terrible momentum of its own. And when we make this necessary distinction between the organized witch-craze and the miscellaneous witch-beliefs out of which it was constructed, we have to admit that the Church of the Dark Age did its best to disperse these relics of paganism which the Church of the Middle Ages would afterwards exploit. Of course it was not entirely successful. Some of the pagan myths, like pagan gods and pagan rites, had crept into the Christian synthesis at an early date and had found lodgement in its outer crannies. St Augustine in particular, with his baroque mind and African credulity, did much to preserve them: they form an incidental bizarre decoration of the huge doctrinal construction which his authority launched into western Christendom. But in general, the Church, as the civilizer of nations, disdained these old wives' tales. They were the fragmentary rubbish of paganism which the light of the Gospel had dispelled.

So, in the eighth century, we find St Boniface, the English apostle of Germany, declaring roundly that to believe in witches and werewolves is unchristian.[1]* In the same century Charlemagne decreed the death penalty for anyone who, in newly converted Saxony, burnt supposed witches. Such burning, he said, was 'a pagan custom'.[2] In the next century St Agobard,[3] Bishop of Lyon, repudiated the belief that witches could make bad weather, and another unknown Church dignitary declared that night-flying and metamorphosis were hallucinations and that whoever believed in them 'is beyond doubt an infidel and a pagan'. This statement was accepted into the canon law and became known as the *canon Episcopi* or *capitulum Episcopi*.[4] It remained the official doctrine of the Church. In the eleventh century the laws of King Coloman of Hungary declined to notice witches 'since they do not exist',[5] and in the twelfth-century John of Salisbury dismissed the idea of a witches' sabbat as a fabulous dream.[6] In the succeeding centuries, when the

* For such references see Notes at end of book.

craze was being built up, all this salutary doctrine would have to be reversed. The laws of Charlemagne and Coloman would be forgotten; to deny the reality of night-flying and metamorphosis would be officially declared heretical; the witches' sabbat would become an objective fact, disbelieved only (as a doctor of the Sorbonne would write in 1609[7]) by those of unsound mind; and the ingenuity of churchmen and lawyers would be taxed to explain away that inconvenient text of canon law, the *canon Episcopi*.

By the end of the Middle Ages this reversal would be complete. By 1490, after two centuries of research, the new, positive doctrine of witchcraft would be established in its final form. From then on it would be simply a question of applying this doctrine: of seeking, finding and destroying the witches whose organization has been defined.

The monks of the late Middle Ages sowed: the lawyers of the sixteenth century reaped; and what a harvest of witches they gathered in! All Christendom, it seems, is at the mercy of these horrifying creatures. Countries in which they had previously been unknown are now suddenly found to be swarming with them, and the closer we look, the more of them we find. All contemporary observers agree that they are multiplying at an incredible rate. They have acquired powers hitherto unknown, a complex international organization and social habits of indecent sophistication. Some of the most powerful minds of the time turn from the human sciences to explore this newly discovered continent, this America of the spiritual world. And the details which they discover, and which are continually being confirmed by teams of parallel researchers — field researchers in torture-chamber or confessional, academic researchers in library or cloister — leave the facts more certainly established and the prospect more alarming than ever.

Consider the situation as shown at any time in the half-
century from 1580 to 1630: that half-century which corresponds with the mature life of Bacon and brings together
Montaigne and Descartes. The merest glance at any report
by the acknowledged experts of the time reveals an alarming
state of affairs. By their own confession, thousands of old
women – and not only old women – had made secret pacts
with the Devil, who had now emerged as a great spiritual
potentate, the Prince of Darkness, bent on recovering his
lost empire. Every night these ill-advised ladies were anoint-
ing themselves with 'devil's grease', made out of the fat of
murdered infants, and, thus lubricated, were slipping
through cracks and keyholes and up chimneys, mounting
on broomsticks or spindles or airborne goats, and flying off
on a long and inexpressibly wearisome aerial journey to a
diabolical rendezvous, the witches' sabbat. In every country
there were hundreds of such sabbats, more numerous and
more crowded than race-meetings or fairs. There were no
less than 800 known meeting-places in Lorraine alone. Some
countries had national, some international centres. Such
were the Blocksberg or Brocken in the Harz Mountains of
Germany, the 'delicate large meadow' called Blåkulla in
Sweden, and the great resort of La Hendaye in south-west
France where no less than 12,000 witches would assemble
for the gathering known as the *Aquelarre*. The meetings
too were remarkably frequent. At first the interrogators in
Lorraine thought that they occurred only once a week, on
Thursday; but, as always, the more the evidence was pressed,
the worse the conclusions that it yielded. Sabbats were found
to take place on Monday, Wednesday, Friday and Sunday,
and soon Tuesday was found to be booked as a by-day. It
was all very alarming and proved the need of ever greater
vigilance by the spiritual police.

And what happened when the witch had reached the

sabbat? The unedifying details, alas, were only too well authenticated. First, she was surprised to observe nearly all her friends and neighbours, whom she had not previously suspected to be witches. With them there were scores of demons, their paramours, to whom they had bound themselves by the infernal pact; and above all, dominating them all, was the imperious master of ceremonies, the god of their worship, the Devil himself, who appeared sometimes as a big, black, bearded man, more often as a stinking goat, occasionally as a great toad. Those present recognized their master. They all joined to worship the Devil and danced around him to the sound of macabre music made with curious instruments – horses' skulls, oak-logs, human bones, etc. Then they kissed him in homage, under the tail if he were a goat, on the lips if he were a toad. After which, at the word of command from him, they threw themselves into promiscuous sexual orgies or settled down to a feast of such viands as tempted their national imagination. In Germany these were sliced turnips, parodies of the Host; in Savoy, roast or boiled children; in Spain, exhumed corpses, preferably of kinsfolk; in Alsace, fricassées of bats; in England, more sensibly, roast beef and beer. But these nice distinctions of diet made little difference: the food, all agreed, was cold and quite tasteless, and one necessary ingredient, salt, for some arcane demonological reason, was never admitted.

Such was the witches' sabbat, the collective orgy and communal religious worship of the new diabolical religion. In the intervals between these acts of public devotion, the old ladies had, of course, good works to do in the home. They occupied themselves by suckling familiar spirits in the form of weasels, moles, bats, toads or other convenient creatures; by compassing the death of their neighbours or their neighbours' pigs; by raising tempests, causing blights or procuring impotence in bridegrooms; and as a pledge of their servitude they were constantly having sexual intercourse with the Devil, who appeared (since even he abhors unnatural vice*) to she-witches as an *incubus*, to he-witches as a *succubus*.

What Gibbon called 'the chaste severity of the Fathers' was much exercised by this last subject, and no detail escaped their learned scrutiny. As a lover, they established, the Devil was of 'freezing coldness' to the touch; his embrace gave no pleasure – on the contrary, only pain; and certain items were lacking in his equipment. But there was no frigidity in the technical sense: his attentions were of formidable, even oppressive solidity. That he could generate on witches was agreed by some doctors (how else, asked the Catholic theologians, could the birth of Luther be explained?); but some denied this, and others insisted that only certain worm-like creatures, known in Germany as *Elben*, could issue from such unions. Moreover, there was considerable doubt whether the Devil's generative power was his own, as a Franciscan specialist maintained ('under correction from our Holy Mother Church'), or whether he, being neuter, operated with borrowed matter. A nice point of theology was here involved and much interested erudition was expended on it in cloistered solitudes. Some important theologians conjectured that the Devil equipped himself by squeezing the organs of the dead. This view was adopted (among others) by our King James.[8] Other experts advanced other theories, more profound than decent. But on the whole, Holy Mother Church followed the magisterial ruling of the Angelic Doctor, St Thomas Aquinas, who, after St Augustine, must be regarded as the second founder of demono-

*Except, apparently, in Alsace. See R. Reuss, *L'Alsace au 17e siècle* (Paris, 1898), ii, 106. Elsewhere 'the nobleness of his nature' repudiates it (Lea, *Materials*, pp. 161, 380).

logical science. According to him, the Devil could discharge as *incubus* only what he had previously absorbed as *succubus*. He therefore nimbly alternated between these postures . . . . There are times when the intellectual fantasies of the clergy seem more bizarre than the psychopathic delusions of the madhouse out of which they have, too often, been excogitated.

Such were the human witches, the fifth column of Satan on earth, his front-line agents in the struggle for control of the spiritual world. All through the sixteenth century, and for much of the seventeenth, men believed in the reality of this struggle. Laymen might not accept all the esoteric details supplied by the experts, but they accepted the general truth of the theory, and because they accepted its general truth, they were unable to argue against its more learned interpreters. So the experts effectively commanded the field. For two centuries the clergy preached against witches and the lawyers sentenced them. Year after year inflammatory books and sermons warned the Christian public of the danger, urged the Christian magistrate to greater vigilance, greater persecution. Confessors and judges were supplied with manuals incorporating all the latest information, village hatreds were exploited in order to ensure exposure, torture was used to extract and expand confessions, and lenient judges were denounced as enemies of the people of God, drowsy guardians of the beleaguered citadel. Perhaps these 'patrons of witches' were witches themselves. In the hour of danger, when it almost seemed that Satan was about to take over the world, his agents were found to be everywhere, even in judges' seats, in university chairs and on royal thrones.

But did this campaign against the witches in fact reduce their number? Not at all. The more fiercely they were persecuted, the more numerous they seemed to become. By the

beginning of the seventeenth century the witch-doctors*
have become hysterical. Their manuals have become encyclopedic in bulk, lunatic in pedantry. They demand, and
sometimes achieve, wholesale purges. By 1630 the slaughter
has broken all previous records. It has become a holocaust in
which lawyers, judges, clergy themselves join old women at
the stake. That at least, if nothing else, must have enforced
an agonizing reappraisal.

And indeed, it was in the wake of the greatest of all purges
– perhaps in revulsion after it – that the solidity of the witch-
hunters began to give way. In the middle of the seventeenth
century – in the 1650s – scepticism, unavailing hitherto,
begins at last to break through. Imperceptibly, the whole
basis of the craze begins to dissolve, in Catholic and Protestant countries alike. By the 1680s the battle is effectively
won, at least in the west. The old habits of mind may linger
on; there will be pockets of resistance here and there, recur-
rence of persecution now and then, but somehow the vital
force behind it is spent. Though the argument may go
on, the witch-trials and witch-burnings have become once
again mere sporadic episodes, as they had been before the
Renaissance. The rubbish of the human mind which for
two centuries, by some process of intellectual alchemy
and social pressure, had become fused together in a coherent, explosive system, has disintegrated. It is rubbish
again.

How are we to explain this extraordinary episode in
European history? In the eighteenth century, when the men
of the Enlightenment looked back on this folly of 'the last
age', they saw it merely as evidence of the 'superstition' from
which they had recently been emancipated, and the nine-

* I use this convenient term to describe the scholars, clerical and lay,
who by their writings formulated, elaborated and defended the persecution.

teenth-century historians, who approached it in a more detached, scientific spirit, interpreted their more abundant material in the same general terms. To the German Wilhelm Gottlieb Soldan,[9] the first historian of the craze, the witch-cult was a legacy of Greco-Roman antiquity, naturally developed, artificially preserved. To him, as to the Englishman W. E. H. Lecky, its gradual conquest was one aspect of the rise of 'rationalism' in Europe.[10] To the American Andrew Dickson White it was a campaign in 'the warfare of science with theology'.[11] But none of these scholars sought to explain why the centuries of Renaissance and Reformation were so much less 'rational', less 'scientific' than the Dark and early Middle Ages. Even the profoundest of nineteenth-century historians of witchcraft, Joseph Hansen, the liberal, free-thinking archivist of Cologne, hardly faced this problem. In two important works[12] he collected a mass of documentary material and presented a lucid narrative of 'the rise of the great witch-craze'; but as he aimed only to document its origins, he concluded his work once he had brought it to the early sixteenth century, when 'the system of the new witch-craze had achieved its final form'.[13] The fact that, in this final form, the craze was to last for two centuries, and those the centuries of Renaissance, Reformation and experimental science, did indeed perplex him. He suggested that the explanation lay in the survival of 'the medieval spirit'. This answer, says the modern historian of magic, is 'unconvincing'.[14] But is his own explanation any more convincing? The witch-craze, says Lynn Thorndike (echoing Michelet[15]), grew naturally out of the misery of the fourteenth century, that century of the Black Death and the Hundred Years War. These disasters no doubt helped; but they do not explain. As Hansen had already observed, the craze gathered force before either of them had begun, and it continued, in its 'final form', for two centuries after both were over: two centuries not of misery, but of European recovery and expansion.

While Hansen was writing about the witch-craze in Germany, another great historian was thinking about it in America. In his youth H. C. Lea had begun a work on 'man's assumed control over spiritual forces' in which he hoped to deal with the whole question of witchcraft in the world; but illness interrupted it, and he afterwards deviated into what he described as the 'bypath' of 'a simpler and less brain-fatiguing amusement'. In other words, he wrote his two monumental works on the medieval and the Spanish Inquisition.[16] But the Inquisition cannot be divorced from the subject of witchcraft and in both works Lea found himself brought up against it. In his history of the medieval Inquisition, he showed the gradual merging of sorcery and heresy, and in his Spanish studies he showed that in Spain, 'thanks to the good sense of the Inquisition', the witch-craze 'was much less dreadful than in the rest of Europe'. It was not till he was eighty-one that Lea returned to his original subject. He collected, annotated and arranged a vast mass of material covering the whole history of witchcraft in Christendom; but when he died, the book itself was unwritten. His material, however, has been edited and published,[1] and his interpretation is clear from his notes, as also from his earlier works.

Lea is one of the greatest of liberal historians. It is inconceivable that his work on the Inquisition, as an objective narrative of fact, will ever be replaced. Its solidity has withstood all partisan criticism. His 'History of Witchcraft', had it been written, would no doubt have stood as firm. Nevertheless, as interpreters of social history, even the greatest of the nineteenth-century liberal historians now seem to date. Their philosophy was formed in the happy years before 1914, when men could look back on the continuous progress, since the seventeenth century, of 'reason', toleration, humanity, and see the constant improvement of society as the effect of the constant progress of liberal ideas. Against such a background it was natural to see the witch-craze of the past, like the persecution of Moors and Jews, or the use of torture, or the censorship of books, as a residue of mere obscurantism which growing enlightenment had gradually dispelled, and which would now never return.

Unfortunately, we have seen them return. With the advantage of after-knowledge, we look back and we see that even while the liberal historians were writing, their olympian philosophy was being threatened from beneath. It was in the 1890s that the intellectual foundations of a new witch-craze were being laid. It was then that *The Protocols of the Elders of Zion* were forged in France and the grotesque mythology of antisemitism was used to inspire the pogroms of eastern Europe. To the liberals of the time this new form of superstition was beneath contempt. At most, it was a lingering survival of past superstition. We who have seen its vast and hideous consequences cannot accept so comforting an explanation. Faced by the recrudescence, even in civilized societies, of barbarous fantasies in no way less bizarre and far more murderous that the witch-craze, we have been forced to think again, and thinking, to devalue the power of mere thought. Even intellectual history, we now admit, is relative and cannot be dissociated from the wider, social context with which it is in constant interaction.

This being so, we are prepared to admit, as our ancestors were not, that mental structures differ with social structures, that the 'superstition' of one age may be the 'rationalism' of another, and that the explanation of intellectual change may have to be sought outside purely intellectual history. We cannot see the long persistence and even aggravation of the witch-craze merely as a necessary effect of clerical domination, or its dissolution as the logical consequence of release from religious fundamentalism. Therefore we may be forgiven for looking at this whole episode, whose basic facts, thanks to the work of our predecessors, are not in dispute, with eyes different from theirs. They saw, through all the centuries, a continuous dialogue between superstition, whose form constantly varied, and reason, which was always the same. We agree with one of the most perceptive and philosophical of modern French historians, that the mind of one age is not necessarily subject to the same rules as the mind of another, that '*dans sa structure profonde, la mentalité des hommes les plus éclairés de la fin du 16ᵉ siècle, du début du 17ᵉ siècle, ait différé, et radicalement, de la mentalité des hommes les plus éclairés de notre temps*'.[17]

2
SOCIAL ORIGINS

WHEN Hansen wrote that the system of the new witch-craze had achieved its final form by the 1480s, he was referring to the two documents of that decade from which the centralized European witch-craze, as distinct from spasmodic local outbursts, can be dated. The first of these is the papal bull *Summis Desiderantes Affectibus*, issued by Pope Innocent VIII in December 1484, deploring the spread of witchcraft in Germany and authorizing his beloved sons, the Dominican inquisitors Heinrich Institor (Krämer) and Jakob Sprenger, to extirpate it. The second is the earliest great printed encyclopedia of demonology, the *Malleus Maleficarum*, 'the Hammer of Witches', published by these same two inquisitors two years later, in 1486. The relationship between these two documents is perfectly clear: they are complementary one to the other. The papal bull had been solicited by the inquisitors, who wished for support in their attempt to launch the witch-hunt in the Rhineland. Having obtained it, they printed it in their book, as if the book had been written in response to the bull. The book thus advertised to all Europe both the new epidemic of witchcraft and the authority which had been given to them to suppress it.

The importance of the papal bull of 1484 is incontestable. Apologists for the papacy have protested that it made no change: it was merely a routine document which authorized the Dominicans to go on doing what they were already doing and told other authorities – bishops and secular powers – not to obstruct their work.[18] No doubt it did this; but it also did something else, which was new. What the Dominicans

had been doing hitherto was local. They had been persecuting and burning witches locally. From now on a general
mandate was given, or implied. And the *Malleus*, which is
inseparable from the bull, gave force and substance to that
mandate. First, by its content, by gathering together all the
curiosities and credulities of Alpine peasants and their confessors, it built up a solid basis for the new mythology.
Secondly, by its universal circulation, it carried this mythology, as a truth recognized by the Church, over all Christendom. Finally, the *Malleus* explicitly called on other
authorities, lay and secular, not merely not to obstruct, but
positively to assist the inquisitors in their task of exterminating witches. From now on, the persecution, which had been
sporadic, was – at least in theory – made general, and secular
authorities were encouraged to use the methods and mythology of the Inquisition. Rome had spoken.

Why did Rome speak? Why did Innocent VIII, that
worldly humanist, the patron of Mantegna and Pinturicchio,
Perugino and Filippino Lippi, yield to these fanatical Dominican friars? The answer, obviously, is not to be sought in
his personality. It is to be sought rather in circumstances:
in the historical situation out of which the witch-beliefs had
arisen and in the war which the Dominican inquisitors had
long been waging against them. This question brings us at
once to a particular area, the area in which these beliefs had
always been endemic and in which, for two centuries, they
had already been persecuted: the mountain areas of Catholic Europe, the Alps and the Pyrenees.

The mountain origin of the witch-craze is by now well
established. So are the circumstances in which it was formulated, and in which the Dominicans came to be its great
adversaries. These circumstances bring us back to the very
foundation of the order, in the struggle between the Catholic
Church and the heretics of the twelfth century, the Albigen-

sians of Languedoc and the Vaudois of the Alps. It was to combat these heretics that the Inquisition and the Dominican order had been founded, and it was in the course of that 'crusade' that the inquisitors had discovered, beneath the forms of one heresy, the rudiments (as they thought) of another. From an early date, therefore, they had pressed the Pope to grant them jurisdiction over witchcraft as well as over recognized theological heresy. To the Dominicans the two forms of error were inseparable: one continued the other, and the pursuit must not cease when the formal error had disappeared underground. They could still recognize it by its smell. So, although the form might seem to change, the old names persisted. By the fifteenth century we hear little of Vaudois or Cathari as theological terms: those errors had been burnt out, at least for a time. But in the Alps, in the Lyonnais and in Flanders witches are known as *Waudenses* and their gatherings as a *Valdesia* or *Vauderye*, and in the Pyrenees we find them described as *Gazarii* or 'Cathars'.[19]

When the Dominicans pressed for inquisitorial power over witchcraft, the papacy had at first resisted. The old canons of the Church, and particularly the *canon Episcopi*, denied the reality of witches and forbade their persecution. Therefore, in 1257, Pope Alexander IV had refused these demands unless manifest heresy, not merely witchcraft, could be proved. But little by little, under constant pressure, the papacy had yielded. The great surrender had been made by the French popes of Avignon, and particularly by the two popes from southern France, John XXII and his successor Benedict XII, who had already, as bishops in Languedoc, waged war on nonconformity in the old Albigensian and Vaudois areas. John XXII, who declared heretical the Franciscan doctrine of the poverty of Christ (so dangerously akin to the old Vaudois ideas), also, by his constitution *Super illius specula* of 1326, authorized the full use of inquisitorial procedure against witches, of whom he lived in personal terror. For the next century and a half – until the Witch Bull of Innocent VIII, and indeed afterwards – the main effort of the inquisitors (although there were some spectacular 'political' witchcraft trials in France, Burgundy and England) had been directed against the witches of the Alps and the Pyrenees.

At first the campaign was most vigorous in the Pyrenees. From the papacy of John XXII onwards, witch-trials were held all over the old Albigensian territory; but soon they spread to the Alps also. The sitting of the Council of the Church in Basel in 1435–7 gave a great opportunity to the local witch-hunters, and it was in those years that a zealous inquisitor, John Nider, wrote what has been called 'the first popular essay on witches'.[20] It was called *Formicarius*, 'the Ant-heap', and was based principally on confessions of Swiss witches collected by a Swiss magistrate, Peter of Berne. The *Formicarius* may be regarded as a little *Malleus*, and it had a similar effect in a more restricted field. Papal instructions were sent out to the witch-inquisitors to redouble their zeal, and in 1440 the deposed Pope, Eugenius IV, took the opportunity to denounce his rival, 'that eldest son of Satan, Amadeus Duke of Savoy' – that is, the successful anti-pope Felix V – as having given himself over to the witches 'or Vaudois' who abound in his land.[21] In the next hundred years some famous inquisitors were busy in the Alpine valleys – Bernard of Como, Jerome Visconti, Bartolomeo Spina. In 1485, according to the *Malleus*, the inquisitor of Como burnt forty-one witches, all of whom confessed to sexual intercourse with *incubi*, and yet even so the practice was increasing. This was the point of time at which the Witch Bull and the *Malleus* were published.

Meanwhile the Pyrenean inquisitors, after a temporary lull, had resumed their activities. In 1450 they too produced a little *Malleus*. This was a tract by Jean Vineti, Dominican inquisitor of Carcassonne: the first work, it seems, to declare that witchcraft was a new heresy, unconnected with the old rural beliefs which the Church of the past had tolerated. This separation of the new witchcraft from the old was a point of great technical importance. Indeed, we can say that it gave the witch-craze its charter: for it enabled the inquisitors to get round the greatest obstacle in the way of witch-persecution: the *canon Episcopi*.[22] About the same time witch-beliefs were found to have spread to the Spanish slopes of the Pyrenees and the King of Castile was invited to take action against them.[23]

Thus by the time that the authors of the *Malleus* obtained the blessing of Pope Innocent VIII, the craze had already been in operation for nearly two centuries in the mountain areas, the old homes of heresy and centres of inquisitorial persecution. The two authors of the *Malleus*, the solicitors of the bull, were themselves natives of the Alpine regions, and all their examples and cases are drawn from upper Germany. The most active of the pair was Krämer, who was inquisitor in the Tyrol; he afterwards became inquisitor in Bohemia and Moravia, where he acted vigorously against the 'Waldenses' of Bohemia as well as against witches.[24]

The Alps and the Pyrenees, the original cradle of the witch-craze, would long remain its base. Individual witches, of course, might be found anywhere, and in certain circumstances might infect whole areas: for the old unorganized superstitions of the countryside were always ready to be inflamed. Isolated rural societies anywhere – in the dreary flats of the Landes in France, or of Essex in England, or in the sandy plain of north Germany – would always be subject to witch-beliefs. Psychopathic disturbances, which could easily be rationalized as witchcraft, are independent of geography. Individual inquisitors, too, would discover or create beliefs in any area in which they happened to operate: Krämer and Sprenger would have plenty of counterparts among the Protestant clergy – and among the laity too, like Matthew Hopkins, the famous 'witch-finder general' of the English civil war. But these are secondary developments, individual extensions. As a continuing social phenomenon, involving not merely individuals but whole societies, the witch-craze would always be associated particularly with the highlands. The great European witch-hunts would centre upon the Alps and their foothills, the Jura and the Vosges, and upon the Pyrenees and their extensions in France and Spain. Switzerland, Franche-Comté, Savoy, Alsace, Lorraine, the Valtelline, the Tyrol, Bavaria and the north Italian bishoprics of Milan, Brescia and Bergamo; Béarn, Navarre and Catalonia: these would be the primary centres. Here the new heresy had been discovered, hence it would be generalized. From the fantasies of mountain peasants, the Dominicans elaborated their systematic demonology and enabled or compelled Renaissance popes to denounce a new heresy in Europe. The heads of the old Albigensian and Vaudois heresy were sprouting again.

This prevalence of witchcraft, and of illusions that can be interpreted as witchcraft, in mountainous areas doubtless has a physical explanation. Rural poverty, as Michelet observed, naturally drives men to invoke the spirits of revenge.[25] The thin air of the mountains breeds hallucinations, and the exaggerated phenomena of nature – the electric storms, the avalanches, the cracking and calving of the mountain ice – easily lead men to believe in demonic activity.[26] But these explanations, by themselves, are not enough. Rural poverty, after all, was a commonplace of all centuries. So, no doubt, were some of the beliefs that it engenders. The superstitions of the mountain are but exaggerations of the superstitions of the plain. Why then, we ask, did the Dominicans wage such war on them? Why did they insist on seeing them as something different from the superstitions which, in the plain, the Church had so long tolerated or ignored? What was the underlying, permanent difference which the Dominicans rationalized as successive layers of 'heresy'?

Sometimes, no doubt, it was a difference of race. The Basques, for instance, were racially distinct from the latinized Germans – Franks and Visigoths – around them. But difference of race, though it may sharpen other differences, is not in itself decisive. It is only when it corresponds with difference of social organization that conflict or incompatibility arises; and then it is the social difference which decides. In the Middle Ages the men of the mountains differed from the men of the plains in social organization, and therefore they also differed in those customs and patterns of belief which grow out of social organization and, in the course of centuries, consecrate it. Theirs, we may almost say, were different civilizations.

Medieval civilization, 'feudal' civilization, was a civilization of the plains, or at least of the cultivated lands which could sustain the manor and its organization. In the poor mountain areas, pastoral and individualist, this 'feudalism' had never fully established itself. Sometimes Christianity itself had hardly penetrated thither, or at least it had not been maintained there in comparable form. Missionaries might have carried the Gospel into the hills, but a settled Church had not institutionalized it, and in those closed societies a lightly rooted orthodoxy was easily turned to heresy or even infidelity. M. Fernand Braudel, in his incomparable work on the Mediterranean, has commented, briefly but brilliantly, on this fact. He has pointed to isolated mountain societies long untouched, or only superficially touched, by the religion of state and easily – if as superficially – converted to the heresy of new evangelists or the

religion of a sudden conqueror. The conversion of the
mountains to Christianity – or, for that matter, to Islam –
(he writes) was far from complete in the sixteenth century;
and he refers to the Berbers of the Atlas mountains, and the
highland Kurds in Asia, so slowly won for Mohammed,
'while the highlands of Spain will preserve the religion of
the Prophet in Christian Spain and the wild Alps of Lubéron
protect the lingering faith of the Vaudois'.[27]

The mountains, then, are the home not only of sorcery
and witchcraft, but also of primitive religious forms and
resistance to new orthodoxies. Again and again they have to
be won back to sound religion; for missionaries come and
go and the established Church does not easily take root in
such poor soil. We see this in England, where the north and
west, 'the dark corners of the realm', would have to be
re-evangelized by Puritan missionaries a century after the
Reformation, and in Scotland, where the Highlands would
relapse into 'paganism' and would need to be recovered by a
new Puritan movement in the eighteenth century. What
would happen in Britain after the Reformation had happened in Europe before it. The Dominicans were the evangelists of the 'dark corners' of Europe where the Catholic
Church was not permanently established. As such they carried the gospel of 'feudal', Christian Europe into the
unfeudal, half-Christian societies of the mountains, and in-
evitably, in that different world, found that their success
was transitory: that ancient habits of thought reasserted
themselves, that social incompatibility clothed itself in religious heresy, and that when formal heresy had been silenced
or burnt out, the same fundamental incompatibility took,
or seemed to take, another form. The old rural superstition,
which had seemed harmless enough in the interstices of
known society, assumed a more dangerous character when
it was discovered, in strange, exaggerated form, among the

barely subdued 'heretics' of the highlands. Thanks to that social gulf, that social unassimilability, witchcraft became heresy.

Once we see the persecution of heresy as social intolerance, the intellectual difference between one heresy and another becomes less significant. Innocent VIII was the persecutor of Bohemian Hussites and Alpine 'Vaudois' as well as of witches, just as John XXII had persecuted Fraticelli as well as witches. Social persecution is indivisible, or at least does not stop at mere intellectual frontiers. But if we wish to see this point more strikingly illustrated, it is useful to turn from one form of Inquisition to another. Only four years before the worldly, humanist Pope, Innocent VIII, yielded to the German Dominicans and launched his bull against the witches of Germany, his predecessor, the even more worldly humanist Pope Sixtus IV, had yielded to the Spanish Dominicans and approved the new Inquisition in Spain. It is difficult entirely to separate these two gestures, so close in time, so similar in consequence, so distinct in place and circumstance; and in fact, by looking at them together, we may be able to shed some light upon them both.

For the Spanish Inquisition, like the medieval Inquisition, was ostensibly set up to deal with formal heresy, and therefore neither the Jews nor the Moors of Spain, at the time of its creation, were subject to it. Heresy is a crime of Christians: the Jews and Moors were then 'unbelievers'. But gradually both Jews and Moors were brought under the control of this organ of social conformity, just as witches had been brought under the control of the medieval Inquisition. The witches had been brought under this control by the device of an extended definition of heresy; the Jews and Moors were brought under that of the Spanish inquisitors by the device of compulsory conversion to Christianity. In both cases the engine of persecution was set up before its future victims were legally subject to it. In both cases, once legally subject to it, the original pretext of their subjection was forgotten. Both witches and converted Jews were first subjected to the Inquisition as heretics; but before long both were being burnt without reference to ideas, the former as witches, the latter as Jews.

Moreover, in both cases the persecutors were the same. It was the Dominicans who, from the start, had persecuted the witches in the Alps and the Pyrenees. It was the Dominicans also who, with some help from the Franciscans, had been the great persecutors of the Jews. This too had been, at first, a sporadic persecution. It had broken out in Germany during the Black Death, when the Jews were accused of poisoning the wells and were burnt in hundreds by angry crowds and petty magistrates. It had broken out in Italy, where the stern Franciscan St Bernardino of Siena had inflamed the mobs against the usurious crucifiers of Christ. From 1391 pogroms had been constant in Spain where the Catalan demagogue, the Franciscan St Vicente Ferrer, had rivalled the exploits of St Bernardino in Italy. The establishment of the Inquisition in Spain was a triumph of the Spanish Dominicans, the expulsion of the unconverted Jews (which left the rest of them subject to the Inquisition) a triumph for the Franciscan Cardinal Ximénez. Both these campaigns can be seen as part of a general evangelical crusade by the friars. That crusade would culminate, in the reign of Innocent VIII's successor, Alexander VI, with the attack on the 'pagan' papacy itself by the Dominican friar Savonarola.

The similarity between the persecution of Jews and the persecution of witches, which reached their climax in different places at the same time, suggests yet again that the pressure behind both was social. The witch and the Jew both represent social nonconformity. At first both are persecuted sporadically, without much reason given; for the witch is not condemned by the old law of the Church, and the Jew, as an unbeliever, is outside it. Then legal grounds are devised to prosecute both: the former by a redefinition of terms, the latter by enforced baptism, are made liable to a charge of heresy. Finally, when that charge is no longer convenient, it is no longer used. The witch, as we shall see, is persecuted simply for 'being a witch', the Jew for 'being a Jew', for reasons not of belief but of blood, for defect of *limpieza de sangre*. Thus the reasons vary but the persecution continues: clear evidence that the real reason lies deeper than the reason given.

Moreover, it sometimes seems that these two types of social nonconformity are interchangeable. In its periods of introversion and intolerance Christian society, like any society, looks for scapegoats. Either the Jew or the witch will do, but society will settle for the nearest. The Dominicans, an international order, hate both; but whereas in the Alps and Pyrenees they pursue witches, in Spain they concentrate on Jews. It is not that there are no witches in Spain. The Pyrenees, after all, are as much Spanish as French, and in the fourteenth and fifteenth centuries, when the Roman Inquisition operated in Aragon, the witches of northern Spain supplied many of its victims. The earliest of all general treatises on witchcraft was written in 1359 by a Dominican inquisitor-general in Aragon,[28] and in the next century Spanish witches – *bruxas* and *xorguinas* – gave as much trouble to the champions of orthodoxy as Spanish Jews.[29] Numerous works on demonology were produced in Spain in the fifteenth and early sixteenth centuries, and Spanish expertise in such matters was exported to other countries.[30] But once the Inquisition had been firmly established, the local order of priority asserted itself. With Jews and Moors on their hands, the inquisitors had very little time for witches, and so they have won glowing tributes for their 'firmness' and 'temperate wisdom' in this respect.[31]

In Germany, on the other hand, the priorities are reversed. There, outside the Alpine regions, there is little or no persecution of witches in the fourteenth and early fifteenth centuries; but those are the years of terrible anti-Jewish pogroms. About 1450 the inquisitors begin to extend the witch-hunt down the Rhine, and this, of course, is the immediate purpose of the *Malleus*.[32] In the sixteenth century the witch gradually replaces the Jew, and in the seventeenth the reversal is almost complete. If the universal scapegoat of the Black Death in Germany had been the Jew, the universal scapegoat of the Wars of Religion will be the witch. There were exceptions to this generalization, of course. The Rostock jurist Dr Gödelmann, for instance, at the end of the sixteenth century, evidently hated Jews more than the witches about whom he explicitly wrote. He would suspend his liberal utterances about the latter in order to vent his hatred of the former: a blasphemous, impious race rightly expelled from their dominions by many Christian rulers.[33] Perhaps he was merely behind the times. And really good Germans (like Luther) would contrive to hate both together: at the close of the sixteenth century the Catholic Elector of Trier and the Protestant Duke of Brunswick would set out to exterminate both. But in general the emphasis fell either on one or on the other. In our own days it has fallen back upon the Jews.

This interchangeability of victims, which suggests that both Jews and witches were persecuted rather as types of social nonconformity than for doctrinal or other given reasons, can be illustrated in many ways. In medieval Hungary, for instance, witches were sentenced, for a first offence, to stand all day in a public place, wearing a Jew's hat.[34] Witchcraft was one of the charges often made against the Jews. But the neatest instance of alternative priorities between the same two social groups is shown by the events on either side of the Pyrenees in the years 1609–10.

In those years there was a sudden panic of denunciation in the old kingdom of Navarre, which had once straddled the Pyrenees but was now divided into two parts, one governed from Paris, the other from Madrid. The King of France, Henri IV, who was also King of Navarre, in response to the clamour of the noblemen and syndics of the Pays de Labourd, issued a commission to the president of the parlement of Bordeaux and to the counsellor of the parlement, Pierre de l'Ancre, to deal with the matter. In four months these energetic officials, both bigoted Catholics, burnt nearly a hundred witches, including several priests. But in describing his triumphs afterwards, and in denouncing the practices which he and his colleague had so gloriously repressed, de l'Ancre did not stop at witches. A whole section of his work is devoted to denunciation of the Jews: their absurd and indecent rites and beliefs, their cruelty, their greed, their poisoning of Christian wells, their forcible circumcision and ritual murder of Christian children. The Jews, says de l'Ancre, 'by their filth and stink, by their sabbaths and synagogues', are so disgusting to God that he has not only withdrawn from them his grace and his promise: he has also condemned them to creep about the world 'like poor snakes', deprived of every kind of office, dignity or public employment. The Jews, he adds, are ordinarily great magicians: they turn themselves into wolves by night; they can never be converted into good Christians. In other words, they behave just like witches.[35]

Thus in French Navarre the stereotype of the enemy of society is the witch: but the Jew is not forgotten. He comes second, to take the fag-end of persecution, or at least of denunciation. On the Spanish side of the Pyrenees the persecution is no less, but the order of priority is reversed. There in this same year, 1609, the Inquisition had achieved one of its great triumphs: the expulsion from Spain, as unassimilable heretics, of the whole Morisco population. Next year, in 1610, the Inquisition in Navarre, where there were no Moriscos, dealt with its local tensions. At a great *auto-de-fe* in Logroño, fifty-three persons were presented. Many of them were Jews, but no less than twenty-nine were presented as witches. But when the Spanish Inquisition reached the humble category of witches, its appetite was already slaked. Of those twenty-nine, six were burnt alive; another six, having died in prison, were burnt in effigy. The remaining eighteen, having confessed and repented, were spared. As Lea remarks, under any other jurisdiction they would have been burnt. And even this relatively merciful sentence led to a commission of inquiry which concluded, in effect, that all witchcraft was an illusion, so that Spanish witches enjoyed thereafter an even greater immunity. As Michelet wrote, the Spanish Inquisition, *'exterminatrice pour les hérétiques, cruelle pour les Maures et les Juifs, l'était bien moins pour les sorciers'*. Having chosen its victims elsewhere, it could afford to overlook the base, even bestial deviations of Pyrenean goatherds.[36]

So, in 1609–10, as in 1478–84, the persecution of witches can be seen as part of the same process as the persecution of Jews. That persecution was not doctrinal: it was not (whatever excuse might be given) because the victims were 'heretics'. It was not launched merely by the personal decision of a bigot in the papal chair. Neither Sixtus IV nor Innocent VIII was a bigot — nor were Leo X and Clement VII, the Medici popes, who continued the process. Nor was the established Church bigoted. In general the established Church was opposed to the persecution. In the 1480s the established authorities — bishops and secular clergy as well as princes and city governments – disliked it. The authors of the *Malleus* found themselves obstructed by the ecclesiastical establishment in Germany and they were reduced to forging the approbation of the University of Cologne.[37] The Archbishop of Trier resisted the bull, declaring that there were no witches in his diocese.[38] (A century later it would be very different.) Even when the persecution was in full swing, the distinction is still perceptible. The Gallican Church would oppose it in France,[39] the Anglican Church in England,[40] the Catholic Church at its headquarters, Rome.[41] The pressure throughout came from a lower level, from the missionary orders who moved among the people, on the sensitive social frontier between differing communities, whether in the heart of a multi-racial society, as in Spain, or in frontier areas, the areas of missionary activity. The popes might authorize, but the pace was set by the tribunes of the people, and the tribunes in their turn responded to popular pressure, seeking a scapegoat for social frustration.

For no ruler has ever carried out a policy of wholesale expulsion or destruction without the cooperation of society. To think otherwise, to suppose that a ruler, or even a party in the state, can thus cut out part of the living tissue of society without the consent of society, is to defy the lesson of history. Great massacres may be commanded by tyrants, but they are imposed by peoples. Without general social support, the organs of isolation and expulsion cannot even be created. The social resentment of the Spanish *pueblo*, not the bigotry of Spanish kings, lay behind the foundation of the Spanish Inquisition. Spanish society approved the persecution of the Jews and welcomed the expulsion of the Moriscos. French society applauded the massacre of the Huguenots in 1572 and their expulsion in 1685. German society supplied Hitler with the means of destroying the

Jews. Afterwards, when the mood has changed, or when the social pressure, thanks to that blood-letting, no longer exists, the anonymous people slinks away, leaving public responsibility to the preachers, the theorists and the rulers who demanded, justified and ordered the act. But the historian must present to it too its share of the account. Individually that share may be infinitesimal but collectively it is the largest of all. Without the tribunes of the people, social persecution cannot be organized. Without the people, it cannot be conceived.[42]

So it was with the persecution of witches. If the Dominicans, by their constant propaganda, created a hatred of witches, they created it in a favourable social context. Without that context their success is inexplicable. But within that context, these tribunes played an essential part. From the very beginning it was they who detected the social pressure. It was they who mobilized it. And in order to mobilize it, they also supplied the mythology without which it could never have become a European movement. To this mythology we must now turn.

3

INTELLECTUAL ELABORATION

THE mythology of the witch-craze, I have suggested, was the articulation of social pressure. In a religious society such articulation generally takes the form of heresy. But before examining any heresy it is useful to ask who in fact articulated it. Was it the heretics themselves, or was it the inquisitors who articulated it for them? This is an important question, applicable to many historic heresies. It applies, among others, to the Albigensians and to the Vaudois. So, when the inquisitors discovered a new 'heresy' beneath the ruins of Albigensianism, we naturally ask the same question. Did they really discover this new heresy, or did they invent it?

It has been argued by some speculative writers that the demonology of the sixteenth century was, in essence, a real religious system, the old pre-Christian religion of rural Europe which the new Asiatic religion of Christ had driven underground but never wholly destroyed. But this is to confuse the scattered fragments of paganism with the grotesque system into which they are only long afterwards arranged. The primitive peoples of Europe, as of other continents, knew of charms and sorcery, and the concept of night-riding 'with Diana or Herodias' survived into the early Christian centuries; but the essential substance of the new demonology – the pact with Satan, the witches' sabbat, the carnal intercourse with demons, etc., etc. – and the hierarchical, systematic structure of the kingdom of the Devil, are an independent product of the later Middle Ages.* All the

* The idea that witch-beliefs were lingering relics of a systematic pre-Christian religion was first advanced by Jacob Grimm, who, in

evidence makes it clear that the new mythology owes its system entirely to the inquisitors themselves. Just as anti-semites build up, out of disconnected titbits of scandal, their systematic mythology of ritual murder, poisoned wells and the world-wide conspiracy of the Elders of Zion, so the Hammerers of Witches built up their systematic mythology of Satan's kingdom and Satan's accomplices out of the mental rubbish of peasant credulity and feminine hysteria; and the one mythology, like the other, once launched, acquired a momentum of its own. It became an established folk-lore, generating its own evidence, and applicable far outside its original home.

How that folk-lore was established is clear enough to any-one who reads the successive manuals of the inquisitors. Fighting against the enemies of the Faith, they had easily divided the world into light and darkness, and having systematized the kingdom of God in a *Summa Theologiae*, what was more natural than to systematize the kingdom of the Devil in a *Summa Daemonologiae*? The method was the same: the only difference lay in the nature of the material. The basic evidence of the kingdom of God had been sup-plied by Revelation. But the Father of Lies had not revealed

his *Deutsche Mythologie* (Göttingen, 1835), argued that the witch-cult was no other than the ancient Teutonic religion. In this form it was refuted by Soldan, who argued that, in so far as it contained pagan concepts, those concepts could be traced to Roman (and so to Greek and Oriental), not to Germanic paganism (Soldan, p. 494). The distinction may be too fine: possibly some of the coarser ingredients, though justified from literary sources, were directly derived from German paganism (see below, p. 114). But however that may be, the demonological system, as distinct from the particular details incorporated in it, is demonstrably scholastic and medieval. The fancies of the late Margaret Murray need not detain us. They were justly, if irritably, dismissed by a real scholar as 'vapid balder-dash' (C. L. Ewen, *Some Witchcraft Criticisms*, 1938).

himself so openly. To penetrate the secrets of his king-dom, it was therefore necessary to rely on indirect sources. These sources could only be captured members of the enemy intelligence service: in other words, confessing witches.

So the Dominicans set to work and their efforts were soon rewarded. Since a system was presupposed, a system was found. The confessions – those disconnected fragments of truth hardly won from the enemy – were seen as the few visible projections of a vast and complex organization, and so every new confession supplied fresh evidence for deduc-tive minds. The same logic which had constructed the great work of the Angelic Doctor would construct a series of demonological manuals confirming and extending each other. The climax, because of its timing and distribution, would be the *Malleus*. When it was published, it carried on its title-page the bold epigraph, *Haeresis est maxima opera maleficarum non credere* ('to disbelieve in witchcraft is the greatest of heresies'). It was the exact opposite of the ruling of the Church in the Dark Ages. Since the ninth century, the wheel had come full circle.

But if the theory of Satan's kingdom, with its hierarchy of demons and witches, rested ultimately on the confessions of witches, how were those confessions obtained? This ques-tion is crucial. If the confessions were freely given, we have to admit at least the 'subjective reality' of the experiences confessed, and then the remarkable identity of those con-fessions, which converted many a sixteenth-century sceptic, becomes a real problem. On the other hand, if the confessions were obtained by torture, that problem hardly exists. The similarity of answers can be explained by a combination of identical questions and intolerable pain. Since some of the most distinguished historians of witchcraft have adopted this explanation,[43] we must clearly examine the whole question of the part played by judicial torture in the trial of witches.

Judicial torture had been allowed, in limited cases, by Roman law; but Roman law, and with it judicial torture, had been forgotten in the Dark Ages. In the eleventh century Roman law had been rediscovered in the west, and torture had soon followed it back into use. In 1252 Innocent IV, by the bull *Ad Extirpanda*, had authorized its use against the Albigensians. By the fourteenth century it was in general use in the tribunals of the Inquisition, and it was used, particularly, in cases of witchcraft, where evidence was always difficult to find. In 1468 the Pope declared witchcraft to be *crimen exceptum* and thereby removed, in effect, all legal limits on the application of torture in such cases. It was not, as yet, used by the secular courts; and Lea points out that certain of the more extravagant and obscene details of witches' confessions do not, at first, appear before secular tribunals, but only before the tribunals of the Inquisition. In other words, they were obtained only by the courts which used torture. But this distinction between lay and clerical practice did not last for long. At the time of the Renaissance the medieval Inquisition was everywhere in decay and, north of the Alps at least, the secular courts had taken over many of its functions. Thus cases of witchcraft in Germany and France were judged by secular lords who had higher jurisdiction. But at the same time the procedures of Roman law were adopted in the criminal law of all countries of western Europe except England. Thus England alone escaped from the judicial use of torture in ordinary criminal cases, including cases of witchcraft.* It may also be observed that some

---

* There were exceptions – e.g. for high treason – and the English common law provided *peine forte et dure*, or pressing to death, for refusal to plead. But these exceptions are not germane to the present argument. There was also some non-judicial torture in ill-regulated

of the more extravagant and obscene details remain absent from the confessions of English witches.† When we consider all these facts, and when we note that the rise and decline of the European witch-craze corresponds generally with the rise and decline of judicial torture in Europe, we may easily conclude that the two processes are interdependent: that the Dark Ages knew no witch-mania because they lacked judicial torture and that the decline and disappearance of witch-beliefs in the eighteenth century is due to the discredit and gradual abolition of torture in Europe. We may also observe that, since torture has been revived in certain European countries, absurd confessions have returned with it.

That this general conclusion is true, is, I believe, undeniable. The evidence supplied by Lea clearly shows that the witch-craze grew by its own momentum; that witches' confessions became more detailed with the intensification of inquisitorial procedure; and that the identity of such confessions is often to be explained by the identity of procedure rather than by any identity of experience: identical works of reference, identical instructions to judges, identical leading questions supported by torments too terrible to bear. This natural inference is also supported by positive evidence. Accused witches often admitted to their confessors that they had wrongly accused both themselves and others, and these admissions are the more credible since they brought no advantage to the accused – unless they were willing, as they

cases: e.g. during the civil wars, when Matthew Hopkins and his assistants used the *tormentum insomniae*. See Wallace Notestein, *A History of Witchcraft in England, 1558–1718* (New York, 1909), pp. 204–5.

† England was unique in another respect too. English witches, unlike those of Europe and Scotland, were not burnt (as for heresy), but hanged.

seldom were, to make a formal retraction, which meant submitting to torture again. Some judges refused to allow testimony because they knew that it had been created by torture and was therefore unreliable; and it was the increasing recognition of this fact which, more than anything else, ultimately discredited the whole science. As Sir George Mackenzie, the Lord-Advocate of Scotland, declared of the Scottish witches who were still being burnt in his time, 'most of all that ever were taken were tormented after this manner, and this usage was the ground of all their confession'.[44]

It might well be. When we consider the fully developed procedure at continental or Scottish witch-trials we can hardly be surprised that confessions were almost always secured. For such a crime, the ordinary rules of evidence, like the ordinary limits of torture, were suspended. For how could ordinary methods prove such extraordinary crimes? As Jean Bodin would write, not one in a million would be punished if the procedure were governed by ordinary laws. So, in the absence of a 'grave *indicium*', such as a pot full of human limbs, sacred objects, toads, etc., or a written pact with the Devil (which must have been a rare collector's piece),[45] circumstantial evidence was sufficient to mobilize the process. And the circumstantial evidence need not be very cogent: it was sufficient to discover a wart, by which the familiar spirit was suckled; an insensitive spot which did not bleed when pricked; a capacity to float when thrown into water; or an incapacity to shed tears. Recourse could even be had to 'lighter *indicia*', such as a tendency to look down when accused, signs of fear, or the mere aspect of a witch, old, ugly or smelly. Any of these *indicia* might establish a *prima facie* case and justify the use of torture to produce the confession, which was proof, or the refusal to confess, which was even more cogent proof and justified even more ferocious tortures and a nastier death.

Of the tortures used, we have plenty of evidence. Basically they were the same throughout the lands of Roman law. There were the *gresillons* (in Scottish *pennywinkis*), which crushed the tips of fingers and toes in a vice; the *échelle* or 'ladder', a kind of rack which violently stretched the body; and the *tortillon* which squeezed its tender parts at the same time. There was the *strappado* or *estrapade*, a pulley which jerked the body violently in mid-air. There was the leg-screw or Spanish boot, much used in Germany and Scotland, which squeezed the calf and broke the shin-bone in pieces – 'the most severe and cruel pain in the world', as a Scotsman called it – and the 'lift' which hoisted the arms fiercely behind the back; and there was the 'ram' or 'witch-chair', a seat of spikes, heated from below. There was also the 'Bed of Nails', which was very effective for a time in Styria. In Scotland one might also be grilled on the *caschielawis*, and have one's finger-nails pulled off with the *turka*s or pincers; or needles might be driven up to their heads in the quick. But in the long run perhaps nothing was so effective as the *tormentum insomniae*, the torture of artificial sleeplessness which has been revived in our day. Even those who were stout enough to resist the *estrapade* would yield to a resolute application of this slower but more certain form of torture, and confess themselves to be witches.[46] Once a witch had confessed, the next stage was to secure from her, again under torture, a list of all those of her neighbours whom she had recognized at the witches' sabbat. Thus a new set of *indicia* was supplied, clerical science was confirmed, and a fresh set of trials and tortures would begin.

It is easy to see that torture lay, directly or indirectly, behind most of the witch-trials of Europe, creating witches where none were and multiplying both victims and evidence. Without torture, the great witch-panics of the 1590s and the late 1620s are inconceivable. But can we ascribe the whole craze, in effect, to torture, as some liberal writers seem to do? Can we suppose that witchcraft had no other basis than the fanaticism and prurience of the inquisitors, spellbound by their own inventions? I must confess that I find this difficult to believe. The problem seems to me more complex than that. If the confessions were merely a response to torture we should have to explain why even in England, where there was no judicial torture, witches confessed to absurd crimes;[47] why the people were so docile in the face of such a mania; and above all, why some of the most original and cultivated men of the time not only accepted the theory of witchcraft, but positively devoted their genius to its propagation. For, as Lucien Fèbvre said, although we may dismiss Henri Boguet and many others as 'imbeciles', we have to stop before the great figure of Bodin : Bodin the Aristotle, the Montesquieu of the sixteenth century, the prophet of comparative history, of political theory, of the philosophy of law, of the quantitative theory of money, and of so much else, who yet, in 1580, wrote the book which, more than any other, reanimated the witch-fires throughout Europe.[48] To turn over the pages of Bodin's *De la démonomanie des sorciers*, to see this great man, the undisputed intellectual master of the later sixteenth century, demanding death at the stake not only for witches, but for all who do not believe every grotesque detail of the new demonology, is a sobering experience. After such an experience it is impossible, absurd, to suppose that the confessions of witches were mere clerical fabrications, imposed upon reluctant victims by instruments of torture.

Nor is the coincidence in time of judicial torture and the witch-craze in any way decisive. When we look closely at the dates, we find that the abolition of torture did not precede but often followed the disintegration of witch-beliefs. Torture was not abolished in Prussia till 1740 (although it had

been brought under strict control in 1714); but the Prussian
Land Law of 1721 had already declared that no belief could
be placed in the pact with the Devil, night-riding to the
sabbat, metamorphosis, intercourse with demons, etc.; and
since the law always lags behind the fact, we can assume that
the belief had already faded.[49] In Bavaria the decisive blow
to the belief was struck by the Theatine monk Ferdinand
Stertzinger in 1766, but torture was not abolished till 1806.[50]
In France witch-beliefs died before the Revolution, torture
after it. In general, it seems clear that it was the growing
disbelief in confessions produced by torture which brought
torture into discredit: in other words, that the disintegration
of witch-beliefs led to the abolition of torture, not vice versa.

What then is the explanation of those confessions, and of
their general identity? When we read the confessions of
sixteenth- and seventeenth-century witches, we are often
revolted by the cruelty and stupidity which have elicited
them and sometimes, undoubtedly, supplied their form. But
equally we are obliged to admit their fundamental 'subjective reality'. For every victim whose story is evidently created
or improved by torture, there are two or three who genuinely
believe in its truth. This duality forbids us to accept single,
comprehensive, rational explanations. 'Rationalism', after
all, is relative: relative to the general intellectual structure
of the time. The sixteenth-century clergy and lawyers were
rationalists. They believed in a rational, Aristotelean universe, and from the detailed identity of witches' confessions
they logically deduced their objective truth. To the 'patrons
of witches' who argued that witches were 'aged persons of
weak brains' whose melancholy natures were exploited by the
Devil, the Rev. William Perkins could reply with confidence
that, if that were so, each would have a different fantasy;
but in fact men of learning had shown 'that all witches
throughout Europe are of like carriage and behaviour in

their examinations and convictions'. Such international con-
sistency, he argued, was evidence of central organization
and truthful testimony.[51] The liberal scholars of the nineteenth century were also rationalists. They knew that, objectively, the confessions of witches were worthless. Therefore they found another explanation of their identity. They
ascribed it to the identity of the questions and the pressure
of torture. But we in the twentieth century are not rationalists
– at least in our approach to human behaviour and human
belief. We do not look only for external causes of identical
expression or identical illusion. We look also for internal
causes, and we find them in human psychology and
psychopathology.

That external suggestion alone does not account for
witches' confessions is clear when we descend to detail.
Again and again, when we read the case histories, we find
witches freely confessing to esoteric details without any
evidence of torture, and it was this spontaneity, rather than
the confessions themselves, which convinced rational men
that the details were true. It was because he had heard confessions given without torture that Paolo Grillandi, a judge
of witches in central Italy in the early sixteenth century, was
converted to the belief that witches were transported bodily
to the sabbat. Bodin too assures us that the confession which
converted him to the science of demonology and inspired
him to become its most formidable propagandist was made
'*sans question ny torture*'; and yet the woman, Jeanne
Harvellier of Verbery near Compiègne, had been remarkably
circumstantial. Not only had she compassed the death of
man and beast: she had also had the Devil for her paramour
for thirty-eight years, during which he had visited her '*en
guise d'un grand homme noir, outre la stature des hommes,
vestu de drap noir*', coming to her by night, on horseback,
booted and spurred, with a sword at his side. She had also

described her visits to the sabbat in copious detail; and here too the detail had exactly confirmed the science of the demonologists: the long and tiring journey which left her utterly exhausted, the adoration of a big black man whom they called Belzebuh, the sexual promiscuity. Bodin admits that such a story seemed strange and almost incredible at secondhand. But he had heard it himself; he was a man of the world; and he was personally convinced of its spontaneity. Who are we to doubt his conviction? [52]

Or take the case of Françoise Fontaine, the servant-girl whose interrogation at Louviers by Loys Morel, *prévôt-général* of Henri IV in Normandy, was discovered and published in full in 1883. Here there was no question of torture: the *prévôt* was a humane man, and the story was elicited by patience, not pressure. And yet the story is the standard story, even down to the details: the visit of the Devil through the window, in the guise of '*ung grand homme tout vestu de noir, ayant une grande barbe noire et les yeux fort esclairantz et effroyables*'; the large promises made; the oppressive solidity of his attentions, the lack of pleasure derived from them, the ice-cold contact. . . . In his introduction to the document, the Vicomte de Moray has shown, from the evidence of the Salpêtrière hospital in Paris, that every detail of Françoise Fontaine's experience has its parallel today: the diabolic *incubus* is only the sixteenth-century form of a kind of sexual hysteria familiar to every twentieth-century psychiatrist. [53]

Only . . . ? No, not quite. For there is, in these numerous sixteenth-century and seventeenth-century cases, one ingredient which has since disappeared: the Devil. Today, every psychopath has his or her private obsession. The supposed *incubi* and *succubi* vary from patient to patient. In the past the neurotics and hysterics of Christendom centralized their illusions around the figure of the Devil, just as the saints and mystics centralized theirs around the figure of God or Christ. So, while the pious virgins, having vowed themselves to God, felt themselves to be the brides of Christ, the less pious witches, having bound themselves to Satan, felt themselves to be his concubines. The former, like St Teresa or Madame Guyon, enjoyed ecstasies of glowing pleasure piercing their inmost entrails as they clung to the mystical body of their Saviour; the latter, like Françoise Fontaine or a hundred others who were dragged before their judges, felt joyless pangs as they lay crushed in the embrace of that huge black figure who '*jettoit quelque chose dans son ventre qui estoit froid comme glace, qui venoit jusques au dessus de l'estomac et des tétins de ladite respondante*'. In the former psychopathic experience was sublimated in the theology of the Fathers, and they might be canonized; in the latter it ran into disorder in the folk-lore of the demonologists, and they might be burnt.*

Here, surely, we see what the Dominican inquisitors had done, what their successors would do. They did not, of course, discover a concealed world of demons, objectively there (as they supposed). They did not even discover a systematic illusion, a false religion of paganism behind the true religion of Christ. Doubtless there were some pagan survivals in witchcraft just as there were some pagan survivals in Christianity. In Lorraine, for instance, the sabbat was ascribed, incidentally, to the old 'high places' of pre-Christian worship.[54] But what was taken over was mere fragments, not a system: it was the inquisitors who supplied the system.

* There is no need to press the comparison: it is obvious to anyone who faces the evidence. Compare, for instance, the evidence in any sexual witch-trial with the evidence given in J. H. Leuba, *The Psychology of Religious Mysticism* (1925) or the grotesque treatises of the sixteenth- and seventeenth-century demonologists with the hardly less grotesque lives of the baroque saints. The point is also made by the Vicomte de Moray, in *Procès-verbal*, pp. lxxxi–lxxxvii.

Nor did those inquisitors invent a purely imaginary system, in the ordinary sense of that verb : they may have used their ingenuity to create the system, but they did not create the basic evidence on which it rested. They found it in the confessions of supposed witches; and as those confessions seemed genuine to the witches who made them, we can hardly blame the inquisitors for supposing them to be genuine too. What was 'subjective reality' to the penitent was 'objective reality' to the confessor. Out of those fragments of truth, spontaneously given if also amplified by suggestion and torture, a total picture of Satan's kingdom could, by logic, by the 'rationalism' of the time, be built up.

Thus the genesis of the sixteenth-century witch-craze can be explained in two stages. First, there is the social tension. Just as systematic antisemitism is generated by the ghetto, the *aljama*, not by the individual Jew, so the systematic mythology of the witch-craze was generated not by individual old women casting spells in scattered villages – these had always been tolerated – but by unassimilable social groups who, like the Jews and Moors of Spain, might be persecuted into outward orthodoxy but not into social conformity, and who therefore became, as the others did not, objects of social fear. It was out of this tension that the frustrated evangelists began to manufacture the new mythology of Satan's kingdom. That that mythology was entirely fantastic need not here concern us. We may merely observe that, in this respect, it is not unique. Some of the ideas and practices ascribed to the Albigensians, and before them to other esoteric sects,* had been no less fantastic, and the absurdity

* Anyone who supposes that the absurd and disgusting details of demonology are unique may profitably look at the allegations made by St Clement of Alexandria against the followers of Carpocrates in the second century A.D. (*Stromata*, III, 5–10), or by St Epiphanius against the Gnostic heretics of the fourth century A.D. (in his *Panarion*),

of inquisitorial demonology should be a salutary warning to us never to trust the accounts which a persecuting society has drawn up of any esoteric heresy with which it is at war. But once the mythology had been established, it acquired, as it were, a reality of its own. Ideology is indivisible, and those who believed that there were devil-worshipping societies in the mountains soon discovered that there were devil-worshipping individuals in the plains. So the second stage of the witch-craze developed out of the first. The new mythology provided a new means of interpreting hitherto disregarded deviations, an explanatory background for apparently innocent nonconformity. Whatever seemed mysterious and dangerous (like the power of Joan of Arc), or even mysterious and merely odd, could best be explained by it. Nonconformists themselves, in search of a sustaining ideology, even deliberately took up the newly revealed doctrines; sadists like Gilles de Raïs dignified their brutalities by giving them a satanic impulse; helpless victims of society clutched at it for relief; and psychopaths coordinated their delusions about its central theme.

In a climate of fear it is easy to see how this process could happen : how individual deviations could be associated with a central pattern. We have seen it happen in our own time. The McCarthyite experience of the United States in the 1950s was exactly comparable : social fear, the fear of a

---

or by St Augustine against certain Manichaean heretics (*c. Faustum*, xv, 7; xxii, 30; xx, 6; *de Moribus*, ii, 65; *de Natura Boni*, 47; *de Haeresibus*, 46); or indeed at the remarks of Tacitus on the early Christians (*Annals*, xv, 44) or of the orthodox Catholics on the Albigensians and Vaudois of the twelfth century and the Fraticelli of the fourteenth (see the remarks of Juan Ginés de Sepúlveda quoted in Lea, *Materials*, p. 203). In these recurrent fantasies the obscene details are often identical, and their identity sheds some light on the psychological connexion between persecuting orthodoxy and sexual prurience. The springs of sanctimony and sadism are not far apart.

different kind of society, was given intellectual form as a heretical ideology and suspect individuals were then persecuted by reference to that heresy. In the same way, in the fourteenth and fifteenth centuries the hatred felt for unassimilable societies was intellectualized as a new heresy and politically suspect individuals were brought to judgement by reference to it. The great sorcery trials in France and England at that time – the trials of the Templars and Joan of Arc, of the Duchess of Gloucester and the Duchess of Bedford – were political exploitations of a social fear and a social ideology, whose origins were to be found at a deeper level and in another field. The difference was that whereas McCarthyism in America lasted only a few years (although it may yet recur), the European witch-craze had a far longer history. The new ideology reached its final form in the 1480s. From the publication of the *Malleus* onwards, its basic content never changed. There was no further development. And yet equally there was no disintegration. It formed a reservoir of monstrous theory from which successive persecutions were fed: persecutions which did not diminish but were positively intensified in the course of the next two hundred years.

4

SUPREMACY

THE duration of the witch-craze is certainly surprising, for whatever forces may have created it there were others which would seem naturally to undermine it. In the fourteenth century, that century of plague and depression and social dislocation, the mental climate might be congenial; * but the later fifteenth century, which saw the craze formally launched, was the beginning of a period of new European expansion. Nor was the craze, even then, firmly accepted. The established Church – the bishops and the secular clergy – had no great love of the friars and their fanatical doctrines. The educated urban laity of Europe were in no mood to swallow the Alpine credulities, the monkish phantasmagoria of excited missionaries. City governments, even in what were to become the classic lands of witchcraft, resisted the craze, with varying success, even at its height. † Civil law-

*The spread of witchcraft in fifteenth-century France is explicitly connected with the devastation of the Hundred Years War by Petrus Mamoris, canon of St Pierre of Saintes and Regent of the University of Poitiers, in his *Flagellum Maleficorum*, written about 1462 and published, without date or indication of place, about 1490 (sig. a ii verso, '*Ingressus ad Rem*').

† Thus the magistrates of Metz, in the witch-ridden duchy of Lorraine, at least resisted the claims of the Dominican inquisitor to be sole judge in 1456 (Lea, *Materials*, p. 235). The Senate of Venice similarly opposed the operations of the Dominican inquisitors in the dioceses of Bergamo and Brescia (see the bull *Honestis petentium votis* of Leo X in 1521; cf. Soldan–Heppe, I, 555–7). The city of Cologne successfully kept down the persecution until 1629 (see p. 83 of the present book). The city of Nuremberg was an island of safety for witches in Bavaria throughout the period (see Burr, *Life,*

yers, the professional rivals of the clergy, were at first highly sceptical of these new doctrines. Besides, the Witch Bull and the *Malleus* appeared in an age of enlightened criticism. It was the time of Renaissance humanism, when Lorenzo Valla and Erasmus and their disciples, under the protection of princes and free cities, were using human reason to dissolve ancient superstitions and established errors. At a time when the older forgeries of the Church were being exposed and the text of Scripture critically examined, why should new absurdities escape scrutiny? Surely the Donation of Constantine and the apostolic authorship of the Apocalypse were not more obviously improbable than *succubi* and the sabbat.*

So we are not surprised to find, at the beginning, a good

p. 185). The city of Strasbourg was another such island in Alsace (see R. Reuss, *La Sorcellerie au 16e et 17e siècles, particulièrement en Alsace*, Strasbourg, 1871, pp. 178–81). The city of Lübeck survived the sixteenth century almost untouched by the craze (Soldan–Heppe, 1, 526–7).

*The attitude of Erasmus towards witchcraft is disputed. His references to it are few, and their interpretation (since he never explicitly affirms or questions its reality) depends on the amount of irony which can be detected in the tone of his voice; which in turn depends on the reader. A letter of 14 January 1501 concerning a sorcerer of Meung-sur-Loire (*Des. Erasmi Opus Epistolarum*, ed. P. S. Allen, 1, 1906, 334–41) has been interpreted as showing scepticism by some (e.g. Thomasius, *de Origine ac Progressu Processus Inquisitorii contra Sagas*, Halle, 1729, pp. 52–3; Soldan, p. 321; G. Längin, *Religion und Hexenprozess*, Leipzig, 1888, p. 73), credulity by others (e.g. Paulus, *Hexenwahn und Hexenprozess*, p. 18, who is followed by Bauer in Soldan–Heppe, 1, 414). But I find it difficult to read Erasmus's accounts of the witches near Freiburg-im-Breisgau, one of whom caused a village to be burnt down, while the other conducted an amour with an inn-keeper's daughter and inundated a village with fleas, as written in a serious spirit. Erasmus himself described such stories as *vulgi fabulas* (op. cit., x, 275, 316, 324). In any case, it is clear that the general philosophy of Erasmus was sceptical, and it seems safer, with him as with Grotius, Selden, deal of dissent. When the Archduke Sigismund of Austria learned of the new doctrines which were to be extirpated from his Tyrolean lands, he invited a learned civil lawyer, a doctor of Padua, now professor in Constance, to give him advice; and the lawyer, Ulrich Müller (alias Molitor), replied with a treatise in which he insisted that although there were witches who listened to the suggestions of the Devil and who therefore deserved to die, nevertheless these witches had none of the powers which they claimed but were the victims of despair or poverty or village hatreds.[55] Such opinions were widely repeated. Lawyers like Andrea Alciati and Gianfrancesco Ponzinibio, philosophers like Cornelius Agrippa of Nettesheim and Girolamo Cardano, medical men like Antonio Ferrari, called Galateo, even Franciscan Schoolmen like Samuel de' Cassini all agreed that the powers

---

Bacon, etc. (see below, p. 109), to deduce his particular views from his known general ideas than to seek to extract evidence of belief from casual and elliptical references.

Moreover, the very silence of Erasmus is expressive. In his Annotations on the New Testament he avoids every opportunity of encouraging the demonologists. On all those passages from which Catholics and Protestants alike deduced the power of the Devil to intervene in human affairs (Matt. iv. 5, Luke iv. 2, Rev. xii. 12), Erasmus is almost ostentatiously unhelpful. '*Diaboli nomen*', he says firmly, in connexion with the temptation of Christ (and the Devil's power to transport Christ to the pinnacles of the Temple was one of the stock proofs of his power to transport witches to the sabbat) '... *non spiritum impium sed simpliciter delatorem aut calumnia-torem significare videtur*.' In this, as in so much else, he is followed by Grotius. And since Erasmus regarded the encounters of the Desert Fathers, Paul and Anthony, with the Devil, though described by St Jerome, whom he revered, as imaginary, he is unlikely to have given more credit to the similar encounters of witches, as described by monks, whom he hated. De l'Ancre, incidentally, included Erasmus among the sceptics whose incredulity had culpably weakened the crusade against witches (*L'Incrédulité*, p. 23), and Weyer, the greatest opponent of the craze, was a disciple of Erasmus. (see below, p. 73).

claimed by witches, or ascribed to them, were largely illusions. They were the hallucinations of melancholy, half-starved persons; they should be interpreted by lay science – the science of medicine and law – not theology; and their proper cure was not fire but hellebore, the classical cure for mere human insanity.[56] Such a view had already been advanced two centuries before by the famous medieval physician of the University of Padua, Peter of Abano, who now became widely quoted by all the enemies of the witch-craze – and as widely attacked by its promoters. Indeed, the University of Padua, the centre of Renaissance science, became the citadel of common sense against the new mythology: its doctors appealed from the new Aristotle of the Schoolmen to the original Aristotle of Stagira, and in that process the philosophical basis of witchcraft dissolved. Agostino Nifo, doctor of Padua and physician to 'el Gran Capitán', Gonzalo de Córdoba, and to Pope Leo X, showed that, in a true Aristotelean universe, there was no room for demons. The greatest of the Paduans, Pietro Pomponazzi, went further. Cautiously, and hedging his meaning with pious lip-service to orthodoxy (for his work on the immortality, or rather mortality, of the soul had already been publicly burnt in Venice), he argued that all the marvels which the vulgar, and the Church, ascribed to demons could be explained away by other influences. Those influences were not yet purely 'natural' forces: they were celestial bodies and hidden powers. But at least they were not diabolic interventions. Pomponazzi maintained that apparitions were natural phenomena and that men 'possessed by the devil' were merely melancholic. 'Had his views prevailed', writes the greatest authority on Renaissance magic, 'there would hardly have been any witchcraft delusion and persecution or religious wars.'[57]

If the revived and purified Aristoteleanism of the Renaissance pointed one way out of the satanic cosmology, another very different way was pointed by the revived Platonism, or rather neo-Platonism, of Florence. The scientific revolution of the sixteenth and seventeenth centuries, it is now generally agreed, owed more to the new Platonism of the Renaissance, and to the Hermetic mysticism which grew out of it, than to any mere 'rationalism' in the modern sense of the word. Ficino, with his 'natural magic', Paracelsus for all his bombast, Giordano Bruno in spite of his 'Egyptian' fantasies, did more to advance the concept and investigation of a regular 'Nature' than many a rational, sensible, Aristotelean scholar who laughed at their absurdities or shrank from their shocking conclusions. It was precisely at the time of the Witch Bull that Platonic ideas were adopted in Italy and it was during the next century and a half that they provided the metaphysical impulse to the exploration of Nature. Nature, to the neo-Platonists, might be filled with 'demons' and charged with 'magical' forces, operating by sympathies and antipathies. It might not exclude the existence of 'witches' – creatures who, by arcane methods, contrived to short-circuit or deflect its operations. But at least it had no need of such vulgar mechanism as particular satanic compacts, with their ridiculous concomitants of carnal intercourse, 'imps', broomsticks and the witches' sabbat. It is no accident that 'natural magicians' like Agrippa and Cardano and 'alchemists' like Paracelsus, van Helmont and their disciples were among the enemies of the witch-craze, while those who attacked Platonist philosophy, Hermetic ideas and Paracelsian medicine were also, often, the most stalwart defenders of the same delusion.*

Thus it might seem that the dogmas so magisterially

* Agrippa and Cardano were both frequently attacked as being themselves witches (e.g. by Bodin and James VI). So was the greatest critic of the witch-craze, Johann Weyer, who had been a pupil of

formulated by the *Malleus* would soon crumble against the
corrosive ideas of the new century. However, they did not.
The sceptics spoke only to be instantly overpowered by the
defenders of faith. Those who deny the existence of *incubi*

Agrippa. Among Weyer's supporters was Dr Johann Ewich, a
physician, who was also an advocate of 'natural magic' (although
both he and Weyer opposed Paracelsus). On the other side, Thomas
Erastus of Heidelberg impartially attacked Paracelsus on medicine, in
his *Disputationes de Medicina Nova Paracelsi* (1572), and Weyer on
witches, in his *Disputatio de Lamiis* (1578), and the Provençal
physician Jacques Fontaine of St-Maximin was equally extreme in his
diatribes against witches and against Paracelsus (see *Jacobi Fontani
Sanmaxitani . . . Opera*, Cologne, 1612, pp. 313–25, '*Magiae Paracel-
sicae Detectio*', and cf. Thorndike, *History of Magic and Experimental
Science*, VI, 554). The French Huguenot Lambert Daneau showed
himself an obscurantist Aristotelean scientist in his *Physice Christiana*
(1580) and an obscurantist witch-hunter in his *de Veneficis . . .
Dialogues* (Geneva, 1574). So did the Dutch Calvinist oracle
Voëtius. The French scholar Gabriel Naudé, in his *Apologie pour
les grands personnages . . . soupçonnez de magie* (Paris, 1625), shows
himself an admirer of the Platonists, Hermetics and Paracelsians and
an opponent of witch-beliefs. The same is true of the English physician John Webster (see his *Displaying of Supposed Witchcraft . . .*
1677). The Englishman Richard Franck, who went on a fishing
expedition to Scotland in 1656–7 and expressed scepticism about
witches, was also a Helmontian naturalist (see his *Northern Memoirs*,
ed. Sir Walter Scott, Edinburgh, 1820, pp. 158–9).

This equation of Platonists and 'natural magicians' with critics of
the witch-craze is not constant and some Platonists – like the 'Cambridge Platonists' Henry More and Joseph Glanvill – were also
believers in witchcraft. But logically it seems to me that Renaissance
Platonism and Paracelsianism were incompatible with the crude form
of witch-belief which had been established on the basis of scholastic
Aristoteleanism. For this reason I am not convinced by the suggestion
of Lucien Fèbvre (*Annales: économies, sociétés, civilisations*, 1948,
p. 13) that Renaissance Platonism, merely because it postulated a
world of demons, positively contributed to witch-beliefs. They were
a very different kind of demon. I am grateful to my friend Mr
Pyarali Rattansi for illuminating discussions on this abstruse matter.

and *succubi*, declared the Dominican inquisitor of Lombardy, Sylvester Mozzolino, '*catholice non loquuntur.*' These lawyers, protested Mozzolino's disciple Bartolomeo Spina, referring to Ponzinibio, are altogether ignorant of theology: they should be prosecuted by the Inquisition as the chief cause of the increase of witches. The robust Dominican Vincente Dodo announced that he would pursue the wavering Franciscan Cassini with a brandished sword. Afterwards the lay judges who inherited the mantle of the inquisitors would speak with the same voice. Perer of Abano and Alciati and Agrippa and all their followers, and all lenient judges, Bodin would write, were themselves witches, inspired by Satan in order to divert attention from their own kind and so enable them to multiply in peace.[58]

All through the sixteenth and seventeenth centuries this dialogue continued. The voice of scepticism – the scepticism of common sense, the scepticism of Paduan science, the scepticism of Platonic metaphysics – was never stilled. Every orthodox writer pays reluctant tribute to it by his hysterical denunciations of the unbelievers thanks to whom witches are multiplying so terribly in the world. Nevertheless, at least until the middle of the seventeenth century, the orthodox always prevailed. Dissent was powerless to stay the persecution. It could hardly be uttered in safety. Romances of chivalry could be laughed out of existence, but no Don Quixote dared to kill, by ridicule, the bizarre novelettes which the grave lawyers and divines of all Europe published about Satan's kingdom.

Why was this? Some explanations easily offer themselves. The new intellectual forces were themselves ambivalent. The humanist spirit might be critical in a Valla or an Erasmus, but it could be uncritical in others to whom the very fables of Greece and Rome were as Holy Writ; and those fables – of Circe, of Pegasus, of the amours of gods with men – could be called in to sustain the witch-beliefs. The pseudo-Aristoteleanism of the Church had the support of a vested interest which the true Aristoteleanism of Padua had not. The gulf between the neo-Platonic demons, which filled and animated all Nature, and the diabolic hierarchy of the inquisitors might be very deep and logically impassable, but to the common eye – and even to some uncommon eyes – it was also very narrow and could be jumped. When Ficino and Pico della Mirandola, Reuchlin and Cardano, Copernicus and Paracelsus, Giordano Bruno and Campanella all believed, or seemed to believe, that men, by arcane knowledge, might make angels work for them and so control the movements of heaven, it was not unreasonable for ordinary men to suppose that witches, by a baser acquisition of power, might make devils work for them and so interfere with events on earth.

However, in matters of ideology, it is not generally the ideas which convince. Between two interpretations of any philosophy it is often external events which make the decision. Therefore if we are to ask why the witch-craze, established in its final form in the 1480s, was proof against all criticism for nearly two hundred years, we should perhaps turn back again from its intellectual content to its social significance. We may begin by considering its history: the timing, in relation to external events, of its great outbreaks.

Once we do this, we soon see that a pattern emerges. The fourteenth and fifteenth centuries had been periods of spectacular individual persecutions, but not, outside the Alps and the Pyrenees, of mass crazes. What we have seen, in those centuries, is the formulation of doctrine on the basis of Alpine and Pyrenean experience and the application of it in particular trials, often of a political character. The Witch Bull and the *Malleus* mark the final presentation of the doctrine and help to extend it beyond its original frontiers. They demand a renewed crusade in the mountain areas, but at the same time they carry it outside those areas and call upon the support of secular as well as clerical authorities. In particular, they extend it, or seek to extend it, to lower Germany: that Germany which is already showing signs of the impending revolt from Rome, and in which the great adversaries of Luther would be the Dominicans.[59]

In the immediately following generation we can see the results. The crusade against the Alpine peoples is renewed. There is intenser persecution in Styria and the Tyrol. Then, from 1500 to 1525, there is a real social war, disguised as witch-hunting, in the Italian Alps. According to the Dominican inquisitor in the diocese of Como, a thousand witches were tried and a hundred burnt in his area every year. In the end the population took up arms and appealed to the bishop. The bishop sent a lawyer to report, and the lawyer convinced himself, and told the bishop, that very few of the persecuted peasants were really witches. In 1520 this crusade in the mountains was extended from the Alps to the Apennines and a long persecution soon began in the diocese of Bologna. Simultaneously it spread to the Pyrenees and Spanish inquisitors set to work in Guipúzcoa and Vizcaya. Meanwhile, in Germany, obedient to the bull, the secular powers began to take up the task which the inquisitors had been powerless to carry out.[60]

But apart from occasional activity in Germany, the first half of the sixteenth century, outside the Alps and Pyrenees, was a period of relative calm. The witch-hunt, it seemed, had passed its peak, or perhaps the sceptics were prevailing. In France, after the spectacular trials of the fifteenth century, witchcraft seemed forgotten.[61] Even in Germany, in spite of the *Malleus* and the inquisitors, the persecution remained slight.[62] Moreover, the law refused to make witchcraft in itself punishable by death. Luther and the Dominicans might vie with each other in credulous ferocity, but the imperial

constitution of 1532, the *Constitutio Criminalis Carolina*, if
it generalized the Roman law against witchcraft, also insisted on the old Roman distinction between the 'good' and
the 'bad' witch. Punishment could only be for harm done
by witchcraft: merely to be a witch was not enough.[63] Even
in Switzerland, in those years, persecution was negligible.
Geneva, that mercantile city, the seat of international fairs
and an educated *bourgeoisie*, had long been free from witch-
trials. In Schwyz they were unknown till 1571. Zürich, under
Zwingli, was mild: Zwingli himself never showed any sign
of belief in witchcraft. Erasmian Basel listened to the witch-
stories of the surrounding mountains with polite amusement.[64]

But if the sceptics thought that they were prevailing, they
were soon to know better. If the Catholic evangelists had
launched the craze, the Protestant evangelists would soon
revive and extend it. Already, in the 1540s, there had been
warning signs. In 1540, in Luther's Wittenberg, four witches
were burnt. On this subject Luther himself was as credulous
as any Dominican, and as he grew older, he contrived to
believe more: *succubi, incubi*, night-flight and all. Witches,
he declared, should be burnt even if they did no harm, merely
for making a pact with the Devil.[65] In Zürich, Zwingli's
successors did not imitate his restraint.[66] In Geneva, Calvin
held the same language as Luther. 'The Bible,' he declared,
preaching to the Elect on the Witch of Endor, 'teaches us
that there are witches and that they must be slain .... God
expressly commands that all witches and enchantresses shall
be put to death; and this law of God is a universal law.'
The law of God was stated most explicitly in Exodus xxii.
18: 'thou shalt not suffer a witch to live.' On this savoury
text the Protestant clergy – Lutheran, Calvinist, Zwinglian –
were to preach, with grim relish, for the next century; and
they did not fail to point out that the law of God, unlike the

law of the Emperor, made no exception in favour of 'the good witch'.[67]

Wherever they went, they carried the craze with them. Like the Dominicans before them, the Protestant evangelists introduced the systematic mythology of the Inquisition into countries which hitherto had known only the disconnected superstitions of the countryside. It was Lutheran preachers who brought the witch-craze in the 1560s into Brandenburg, Württemberg, Baden, Bavaria, Mecklenburg. It was they who first carried it into Denmark.[68] Calvinist missionaries who implanted it in Transylvania.[69] It was the Calvinist revolution which brought the first witch-law to Scotland in 1563 and thus inaugurated a century of terror. In the previous year the first general witch-law had been passed by the English Parliament. In both Scotland and England the pressure came from the 'Marian exiles' – the Protestant clergy who, in the days of persecution, had sat at the feet of Calvin or other Reformers, in Switzerland and Germany.*

The responsibility of the Protestant clergy for the revival of the witch-craze in the mid-sixteenth century is undeniable. It has led some commentators to argue that Protestantism has a special responsibility for such beliefs. But this is absurd:

* Notestein, *History of Witchcraft in England*, pp. 14–18, 46, points out that the first prosecutions under the new law were explicitly related, by the magistrate concerned, to the opinions brought by Jewel from Switzerland: 'there is a man of great cunning and knowledge come over lately unto our Queen's Majesty which hath advertised her what a company and number of witches be within England; whereupon I and other of her Justices have received commission for the apprehending of as many as are within these limits'. The Scottish witch-law, according to John Knox, was also passed to 'please the godly' – i.e. his own party – and was enforced by the Protestant lords, his patrons: see his *History of the Reformation in Scotland*, ed. W. Croft Dickinson, 1949, II, 79, 85, 150. Knox was then fresh from Geneva. He showed his own zeal by preaching against a condemned witch in St Andrews in 1572. She was tied to a pillar in the church,

it is to judge on far too narrow a basis. To dispose of such a conclusion, we need only look back to the Dominicans. We may equally look forward to the Jesuits.

For if the Dominicans had been the evangelists of the medieval Counter-Reformation, the Jesuits were the evangelists of the sixteenth-century Counter-Reformation, and if Protestant evangelists carried the craze to the countries which they conquered for Reform, these Catholic evangelists carried it equally to the countries which they reconquered for Rome. Some of the most famous of Jesuit missionaries distinguished themselves in propagating the witch-craze : St Peter Canisius, the apostle of Germany; Peter Thyraeus, the oracle of the witch-burning Archbishop of Mainz; Fr Schorich, the court-preacher of the Duke of Baden; Gregor von Valentia, the theologian of Ingolstadt; Jerome Drexel, court-preacher to the insatiable Duke of Bavaria; Georg Scherer, the court-preacher of the Emperor in Vienna. It was the Catholic reconquest which brought the witch-craze in a terrible form to Bavaria, where dukes William V and Maximilian I, great patrons of the Jesuits, kept the witch-fires burning. It was the Catholic reconquest which decimated the Rhineland in the 1590s, and the Jesuits who stood behind its greatest executioners, the Archbishop of Trier and his terrible suffragan, Bishop Binsfeld. It was the Catholic reconquest which introduced witch-burning into Flanders, and the Jesuit del Rio who would keep it up. Philip II's

---

to hear him, before being tied to the stake, to be burnt (*The Autobiography and Diary of Mr James Melville* (Wodrow Society, 1842), p. 58.

It may be added that the first manual of witch-beliefs to be published in England also came from Switzerland. It was Lambert Daneau's *de veneficis . . . Dialogus*, of which Thomas Twyne published a translation in 1575. Daneau's work had been written at Gien, near Orléans, where he was a Huguenot pastor; but it was published in Geneva, whither he had fled after the massacre of St Bartholomew and where he had formerly learned his doctrines from Calvin himself.

letters patent of 1590, declaring witchcraft the scourge and destruction of the human race, inaugurated a long reign of terror in Flanders. The Counter-Reformation brought the witch-craze to Poland as the Reformation had brought it to Hungary. The restitution of clerical power in 1600 led to the renewal of witch-trials in Franche-Comté. Special powers granted by the Pope in 1604 enabled the Duke Maximilian to intensify the crusade in Bavaria. Pierre de l'Ancre, the gleeful executioner of the Pays de Labourd in 1609, gloried in his Jesuit education.[70]

Thus, if we look at the revival of the witch-craze in the 1560s in its context, we see that it is not the product either of Protestantism or of Catholicism, but of both: or rather, of their conflict. Just as the medieval Dominican evangelists had ascribed witch-beliefs to the whole society which resisted them, so both the Protestant and Catholic evangelists of the mid sixteenth century ascribed the same beliefs to the societies which opposed them. The recrudescence of the absurd demonology of the *Malleus* was not the logical consequence of any religious idea: it was the social consequence of renewed ideological war and the accompanying climate of fear. The parties drew on a mythology which was already there, elaborated out of a similar situation by their medieval predecessors. Perhaps, on the eve of the Reformation, that mythology was on the way out. Who can say what might have happened if Erasmus had triumphed instead of Luther and Loyola? Then the Renaissance might have led direct to the Enlightenment and the witch-craze have been remembered as a purely medieval lunacy. But that was not to be. The frontal opposition of Catholics and Protestants, representing two forms of society incompatible with each other, sent men back to the old dualism of God and the Devil, and the hideous reservoir of hatred, which seemed to be drying up, was suddenly refilled.

The recrudescence of the witch-craze from about 1560 can be documented from innumerable sources. We can trace it geographically, watch it, country by country, as the Protestant or the Catholic missionaries declare war on the obstinate. We can see it in literature, in the series of grotesque encyclopedias in which writer after writer repeated and amplified the fantasies of the *Malleus*. We can see it in its legal form, in the gradual change of law and practice to meet the alleged multiplication of witches, and in the gradual acquiescence of the lawyers in a new and profitable branch of their business.* One of the new practices was the 'cold-water test', the throwing of a suspected witch into a pond or river to see whether she would float or not.† If she did, diabolic aid was proved and she was burnt as a witch. If she sank, innocence could be presumed, although perhaps, by that time, she had drowned. The literature of the time shows that this test was invented, or revived, in the 1560s.[71] At the same time the law itself received an important modification: under clerical pressure it abandoned the old and humane distinction between the 'good' and the 'bad' witch.

In 1563 the Scottish witch-law, obedient to the voice of Calvin, prescribed death for all witches, good or bad, and for those who consulted them.[72] In 1572 Augustus the Pious,

* It is interesting to observe the change in the legal attitude towards witchcraft in the course of the sixteenth century. At first the lawyers were generally hostile to the new mythology – as Mozzolino (see above, p. 61), Francisco de Vitoria (*Relectiones XII Theologicae*, ch. x, cited in Hansen, *Quellen*, pp. 354–7) and others admit. But from mid-century they generally support the witch-hunters, and by 1600 they are more savage and pedantic than the clergy. The same conservative spirit which had once resisted the novelty now venerated the established doctrine.

† So called to distinguish it from the 'hot-water test', which involved thrusting the suspect's arm into boiling water and measuring guilt or innocence by the effect.

Elector of Saxony, introduced a new criminal code, the *Consultationes Saxonicae*, according to which even the 'good' witch was to be burnt, merely for having made a pact with the Devil, 'even if she has harmed nobody with her sorcery'. This provision was the result of organized pressure by the lawyers and clergy of Luther's Wittenberg.[73] The same provision was adopted ten years later in the Palatinate by its Lutheran Elector Ludwig, and by a number of other princes. Where the Catholic, Lutheran or Calvinist Churches ruled the practice was the same.[74] In Elizabethan England the law preserved the old distinction and indeed the Anglican Church has an honourable record of sanity and moderation.[75] Its teacher had been Bucer, the disciple of Erasmus, whose influence also kept Strasbourg as an island of sense in the Rhineland. But even in England the Calvinist clergy pressed for conformity with the pure 'schools of Christ' abroad. Their oracle was the Cambridge preacher and casuist William Perkins, who lectured on the subject in Emmanuel College in the 1590s. He impressed upon his hearers – and indirectly on the founding fathers of New England Puritanism, who were to prove apt pupils [76] – the standard view of the godly that by the law of Moses, 'the equity whereof is perpetual', and from which there are no exceptions, the witch must be put to death. Whoever has made a pact with the Devil, even to do good, must die. Indeed, said Perkins, 'the good witch' was 'a more horrible and detestable monster than the bad'; so if 'death be due to any', as we know that it is due to all, 'then a thousand deaths of right belong to the good witch'.[77] A few years later, the royal demonologist, James VI of Scotland, came to reign in England. Brought up as a good Calvinist and committed to all the absurdities of continental science, he did not like the mild Elizabethan law. He 'found a defect in the statutes', we are told, '. . . by which none died for witchcraft but they only who by that means killed, so that such were executed rather as murderers than witches.' So he had the law changed. Henceforth death was the legal penalty, even in England, for the 'good' witch.[78]

That this recrudescence of the witch-craze in the 1560s was directly connected with the return of religious war is clear. It can be shown from geography: every major outbreak is in the frontier-area where religious strife is not intellectual, a dissent of opinion, but social, the dissidence of society. When Bishop Palladius, the Reformer of Denmark, visited his diocese, he declared those who used Catholic prayers or formulas to be witches; and witches, he said, 'in these days of pure Gospel-light', must be burnt.[79] When Bishop Jewel, fresh from Switzerland, told Queen Elizabeth that witches and sorcerers 'within these last few years are marvellously increased within this your Grace's realm', and demanded action against them, he was declaring Protestant war on the Catholic England of Mary Tudor.[80] The persecution in England was sharpest in Essex and in Lancashire – two counties where Catholicism was strong and the Puritan evangelists particularly energetic. The Scottish Calvinists, when they obtained their witch-law, were similarly declaring war on Catholic society. Germany and Switzerland were also countries where the two religions faced each other in sharp social opposition: in Germany the persecution remained most persistent in Westphalia, the seat of medieval heresy and sixteenth-century Anabaptism,[81] while in Switzerland the Calvinist cities made war on the obstinate peasantry of the country.[82] In France the geographical antithesis was no less clear. The same areas which had accepted the medieval heresies became, in the sixteenth century, the solid base of the Huguenots: in the Wars of Religion the Protestant south opposed the Catholic north and the last redoubt of Protestantism was the last redoubt of Albigensianism,

Languedoc. It was therefore natural that witches should be found in Protestant islands like Orléans or Normandy; that by 1609 the entire population of 'Protestant' Navarre should be declared to be witches; [83] and that the capital of the witch-burners should be the great centre of vindictive Catholic orthodoxy, Toulouse.*

The same connexion can be shown from chronology. The recrudescence in the 1560s marks the period of Protestant evangelism. Thereafter, almost every local outbreak can be related to the aggression of one religion upon the other. The

---

* Toulouse has preserved a constant character of intolerance. It was the centre from which the Albigensian heresy was exterminated; it played a sanguinary part in the suppression of the Huguenots of Languedoc; and it was no less brutal in the war against witches. The first witch known to have confessed to sexual intercourse with the Devil was burnt in Toulouse in 1275 (Lea, *Inquisition in the Middle Ages,* 111, 384). From the time of Pope John XXII, it was the scene of continual and ferocious witch-trials (Lea, *Materials,* pp. 222, 230–32, etc.); and in the single year 1577, according to Pierre Grégoire, a civil lawyer of Toulouse (*Syntagma Juris Universi . . .* , Lyon, 1582), the parlement of Toulouse burnt 400 witches. The same authority would burn Giulio Cesare Vanini for intellectual heresy in 1619 and break Jean Calas on the wheel for being a Huguenot in 1762. The cathedral of Albi, the University of Toulouse, and the thaumaturgical apparatus of Lourdes mark the successive triumphs of an intolerant orthodoxy over spirit, mind and common sense.

The same character of intolerance, regardless of the nature of the heresy, can be detected in Bavaria. The oppressive nature of the Counter-Reformation in Bavaria is well known. Max Bauer, the editor of Soldan–Heppe's *Geschichte der Hexenprozesse,* printed as motto to the book a peculiarly revolting song of Bavarian orthodoxy:

> *Die Teutschen wurden wohlgemut,*
> *Sie giengen in der Ketzer Plut*
> *Als wers ein Mayentawe.*

(The Germans were high-spirited: they waded in the blood of heretics as though it were summer dew.) In our time Bavaria was the cradle of Nazism.

Wars of Religion introduce the worst period of witch-persecution in French history. The outbreak in the Basque country in 1609 heralds the Catholic reconquest of Béarn. The terrible outbreaks in Germany, in Flanders and the Rhineland in the 1590s, and again in 1627-9, mark the stages of Catholic reconquest. Understandably, the Catholic historians of Germany dwell with unction on the persecutions of the 1560s and 1570s, when the witch-burners were Protestant.[84] Protestants can take their revenge by looking back to the Dominican campaign of the later Middle Ages, or forward to the Catholic triumphs of the early seventeenth century.

Was there any difference between the Catholic and the Protestant craze? Theoretically, yes. The Catholics inherited the whole medieval tradition of the later Fathers and the Schoolmen while the Protestants rejected everything which a corrupt papacy had added to the Bible and the primitive Fathers. Theoretically, therefore, they should have rejected the whole demonological science of the Inquisitors; for no one could say that *succubi* and *incubi*, 'imps' or werewolves, cats or broomsticks were to be found in the Bible. This point was constantly made by isolated Protestant critics, but it had no effect on their official theorists. Some Calvinist writers might be more intellectual and austere in detail,[85] but in general Catholics and Protestants vied with each other in credulity. The authority of Luther transmitted all the fantasies of the Dominicans to his disciples, and the confessions of witches were regarded as an untainted supplement to Holy Writ. So, in the end, Catholics and Protestants agreed on the facts and drew on each other for details. The Catholic Binsfeld cites the Protestants Erastus and Daneau; the Calvinist Voëtius and the Lutheran Carpzov cite the Dominican *Malleus* and the Jesuit del Rio. They all also agreed in denouncing those infamous sceptics who insisted on telling

them that supposed witches were merely deluded, 'melancholic' old ladies and that the Bible, in advocating death for
'witches', had not referred to persons like them. From either
side, terrible denunciations fell upon these neuters in
the holy war, these 'patrons of witches', who, together
with lenient judges, were regularly declared to be witches
themselves, equally deserving of the bonfire and the stake.

And who were these sceptics? The most famous of them
was Johann Weyer, a survivor from the civilized days of
Erasmus, a pupil of the Platonist Cornelius Agrippa of Nettesheim, a doctor of medicine who had studied in the humanist France of François I and practised in Erasmian Holland.
In 1550 he had been invited to Cleves by the tolerant,
Erasmian Duke of Cleves-Jülich-Berg-Marck, William V,[86]
and it was under his protection, and with his encouragement,
that he wrote, in 1563, at the age of forty-eight, his famous,
or notorious work, *de Praestigiis Daemonum*. In this, while
accepting the reality of witchcraft and the whole Platonic
world of spirits, he argued that all the activities to which
witches confessed, and for which they were now being burnt
throughout Germany, were illusions created in them either
by demons or by disease. Having written his work, Weyer
sent copies to his friends and awaited the reaction.

The reaction was formidable. Weyer had chosen to pub-
lish his book precisely at the moment when the witch-craze,
after a long lull, was beginning again. That, indeed, was
what had provoked him to write. But this Erasmian Platonist – 'the father of modern psychiatry' as he has been called
– was no longer heard by a generation that had repudiated
Erasmus. A fellow-physician might hail him as a prophet of
enlightenment, a Hercules triumphant over superstition,[87]
but his other readers thought differently. Weyer was told by
his friends that his book must be destroyed or rewritten; by
his enemies that he was a 'Vaudois', a Wycliffite, a lunatic.

His work was denounced by the French Calvinist Lambert Daneau, burnt by the Lutheran University of Marburg, and put on the Index by the Catholic governor of the Netherlands, the Duke of Alba, who would ultimately secure Weyer's dismissal from the Court of Cleves. However, the book was read, and in 1577 Weyer published a sequel in which he congratulated himself on its salutary effect. Unfortunately, he had to add, the tyrants had now resumed their murderous persecution, and so he sought, once again, to expose their errors. This second book happened to come into the hands of Jean Bodin just as Bodin was working himself into a lather of indignation at the leniency of French judges and the infamous neutrality of the French court: the 'Erasmian', 'Platonic' court of Catherine de Médicis.[88] As if he had not written rubbish enough, Bodin hastily added an appendix denouncing Weyer as an infamous patron of witches, a criminal accomplice of the Devil.

There were sceptics after Weyer, but none of them improved materially on his work. Just as the demonology of the witch-hunters, Catholic or Protestant, was laid down in final form in the *Malleus*, so the basic philosophy of the sceptics, Catholic or Protestant, was laid down by Weyer, and neither the one nor the other was modified by the argument of a century. Every champion of demonological science from Daneau and Bodin onwards took care to attack the 'vain ravings' of Weyer; no sceptic, at least in print, did more than repeat his arguments. The most famous of his successors, the Englishman Reginald Scot, if he was inspired by his own experiences, accepted the arguments of Weyer, and thereafter Weyer and Scot feature together, as an infamous couple, in the books of the orthodox. King James VI of Scotland himself wrote his treatise on *Demonologie* to refute Weyer and Scot; when he came to the English throne one of his earliest acts was to have Scot's work sent to the bonfire; and the Dutch Calvinist Voëtius, equally enraged against both sceptics, is able to dismiss their arguments by appealing to unassailable authority: Weyer was refuted by King James and Scot 'by the public burning of all copies of his book'.[89]

The enemies of Weyer, Scot and other sceptics always accused them of denying the reality of witchcraft. Their defenders impatiently insisted that this was not true. Nor was it. Weyer believed implicitly in the power of Satan, but not that old women were his agents. 'Truly I deny not that there are witches', Scot had written, '... but I detest the idolatrous opinions conceived of them.' To the end of the witch-craze, although we always hear it said that there are some who disbelieve the very existence of witches,* we never actually hear the denials. To the last the most radical argument against the witch-craze was not that witches do not exist, not even that the pact with Satan is impossible, but simply that the judges err in their identification. The 'poor doting women', as Scot called them, who are haled before the law courts, and who may confess − whether through torture or delusion − to being witches, have not in fact made any pact with the Devil, or surrendered to his charms, or harmed man or beast. They are 'melancholic'. This was a very tiresome doctrine, and it drove successive orthodox commentators into tantrums of indignation. It could not be refuted. But equally it could not refute the witch-craze. Logically, it left it untouched.

* 'Witches, if there be such creatures' is a phrase which crops up in casual records − e.g. in the remarks of an English soldier in Scotland (see *Letters and Papers illustrating the Relations between Charles II and Scotland in 1650*, Scottish History Society, 1894, p. 136). Edward Fairfax, in *A Discourse of Witchcraft* ... (1621), refers to such as 'think that there be no witches at all', of whom he has heard that there are many, 'some of them men of worth, religious and honest'. But this absolute disbelief is not found in reasoned writing.

The powerlessness of the critics, a full century after the Witch Bull, is clearly shown by the terrible events which accompanied the Catholic reconquest in Germany. If the Protestant princes and petty lords had waged war on witches in Württemberg and Baden, Brandenburg and Saxony, in the 1560s, 'out of respect for law and evangelic piety',[90] the Catholic princes and prince-bishops (who exercised the same power) outdid them in their turn from 1580 onwards. In one German state after another the hunt was then taken up, and no prince was too insignificant to qualify for the competition. The Prince-Abbot of Fulda, for instance, Balthasar von Dernbach, had been driven out by his Protestant subjects. When he came back in 1602, he took his revenge. He gave a free hand to his minister, Balthasar Ross, who styled himself *Malefizmeister* or 'witchmaster' and conducted 'a travelling inquisition' round the principality, falling unexpectedly on villages where he scented a rich prey. He invented new tortures, was paid by results, and in three years, out of 250 victims, had made 5393 gulden.[91] Other instances could be given. But perhaps the most spectacular example, in those first years of reconquest, was given by the pious Archbishop-Elector of Trier, Johann von Schöneburg.

Johann von Schöneburg began his reign in 1581. 'Wonderfully addicted' to the Jesuits, for whom he built and endowed a splendid college, he showed his devotion in militant fashion too. First he rooted out the Protestants, then the Jews, then the witches: three stereotypes of nonconformity. Thanks to his patronage the campaign of Trier was 'of an importance quite unique in the history of witchcraft'. In twenty-two villages 368 witches were burnt between 1587 and 1593, and two villages, in 1585, were left with only one female inhabitant apiece.[92] Among the victims were men, women and children of noble birth and public position. Such was Dietrich Flade, rector of the university and chief judge

of the electoral court. Unconvinced by the confessions which
had been extracted by torture, he judged the victims leni-
ently. Consequently the prince-archbishop had him arrested,
accused of witchcraft himself, tortured till he confessed
whatever was put to him, strangled and burnt. This put a
stop to leniency by judges, and the population of Trier
continued to shrink. As it shrank, the executioner, like some
solitary cannibal, swelled in pride and sleekness, and rode
about on a fine horse, 'like a nobleman of the court, dressed
in silver and gold, while his wife vied with noblewomen in
dress and luxury'.[93]

The craze in Trier was spectacular; but it was by no
means isolated. All through the Rhineland and in south
Germany, in those years, the example was followed, and the
unrestrained secular and clerical jurisdiction of the princes
was capable of terrible abuse. Moreover, like the good kings
of Israel whom they strove to emulate, each prince also had
his prophet to fire his zeal and keep it on fire. The Archbishop of Trier had his suffragan Peter Binsfeld, whose two
sanguinary works, published in 1589 and 1591, were of great
help in sustaining and guiding the persecution. The Archbishop of Mainz had his Jesuit Peter Thyraeus, who went to
press in 1594. The Duke of Lorraine had the lawyer
Nicholas Rémy, whose *Daemonolatreia*, published in 1595,
was hailed as the greatest Catholic encyclopedia of witchcraft since the *Malleus*. The Cardinal-Archbishop of
Besançon in the Spanish Franche-Comté had another lawyer,
Henri Boguet, whose *Examen des sorciers* was published in
1602, its soundness attested by the rector of the Jesuit College
of Besançon. Meanwhile the Spanish authorities in Flanders
were encouraged by the huge success of their local product.
This was the massive encyclopedia of Martín del Rio,
Spaniard turned Fleming, lawyer turned Jesuit. It was first
published in 1599–1600, at Louvain, and quickly replaced

Rémy's work as the new Catholic *Malleus*. When we consider that these same years, 1580 to 1602, the years from Bodin to Boguet, also saw the Protestant *Demonologie* of King James in Scotland, the work of the Calvinist Perkins in England, the translation of Bodin's work into Latin by the Dutch Calvinist Franciscus Junius,[94] and the Lutheran manuals of Henning Gross in Hanover and Johann Georg Gödelmann in Mecklenburg, as well as a hundred lesser works, we see what batteries of learning were ready to quench the thin and feeble voice of dissent.

To read these encyclopedias of witchcraft is a horrible experience. Each seems to outdo the last in cruelty and absurdity. Together they insist that every grotesque detail of demonology is true, that scepticism must be stifled, that sceptics and lawyers who defend witches are themselves witches, that all witches, 'good' or 'bad', must be burnt, that no excuse, no extenuation is allowable, that mere denunciation by one witch is sufficient evidence to burn another. All agree that witches are multiplying incredibly in Christendom, and that the reason for their increase is the indecent leniency of judges, the indecent immunity of Satan's accomplices, the sceptics. Some say, writes Binsfeld, that the increase of witches is an argument for leniency. What a suggestion! The only answer to increased crime is increased punishment: as long as there are witches, enchanters, sorcerers in the world, there must be fire! fire! fire! Rémy thought that not only the lawyers but also the law was too mild. By law, children who were said to have attended their mother to the sabbat were merely flogged in front of the fire in which their parent was burning. Rémy would have had the whole seed of witches exterminated, and pointed (to show that Catholics too could quote the Bible) to the fate of the irreverent children whom Elisha had very properly caused to be devoured by bears. Boguet was reduced to an agony of hysteria when he thought of the fate of Christendom unless the epidemic were checked. Already, he calculated, the witches of Europe could raise an army bigger than that which Xerxes had led into Europe. And all around him he saw signs of their increase. Germany was almost entirely occupied in building bonfires for them – he was looking, no doubt, towards Trier and Mainz. Switzerland had had to wipe out whole villages in order to keep them down – in the last decade at least 311 witches had been burnt, in steadily increasing batches, in the Pays de Vaud alone.[95] Travellers in Lorraine might see thousands and thousands of stakes – the stakes to which Nicolas Rémy was sending them. 'We in Burgundy are no more exempt than other lands. . . . Savoy has not escaped this pest': indeed, it was from the mountains of Savoy that witches descended into Franche-Comté–Savoy, at the Calvinist Daneau had written, which could produce an army of witches able to make war and defeat great kings.[96] All over Europe, cried Boguet, 'that miserable and damnable vermin' was 'multiplying on the land like caterpillars in a garden . . . I wish they all had but one body, so that we could burn them all at once, in one fire!'

When we read these monstrous treatises, we find it difficult to see their authors as human beings. And yet, when we look at their biographies, what harmless, scholarly characters they turn out to be! Rémy was a cultivated scholar, an elegant Latin poet, the devoted historian of his country. When he died in 1616, having sent (we are told) between two and three thousand victims to the stake, he was universally respected. His dedication of his *Daemonolatreia* to Cardinal Charles of Lorraine showed touching personal solicitude: the cardinal suffered from rheumatism, which he ascribed to the machinations of witches.[97] Boguet was similarly a scholar, widely read in the classics and in history. De l'Ancre, the hammer of the Basque witches, is an enchanting writer who gives us an idyllic account of his country house at Loubens, with its grotto and chapel of oyster-shells, poised on a hill overhanging the Garonne, 'the Mount Parnassus of the Muses'. This old antisemite and witch-burner, who had retired thither to devote himself to the Muses, was desolated when gout detained him at Bordeaux and prevented him from showing his 'chapel of grottos and fountains' to Louis XIII.[98] The Jesuit del Rio was also a universally respected figure, dedicated to quiet scholarship from his earliest days, when he had provided himself with a specially constructed combination of desk and tricycle in order to dart, with all his papers, from folio to folio in great libraries. Thanks to such labour-saving devices, he produced an edition of Seneca at the age of nineteen, citing 1100 authorities, and was hailed by no less a scholar than Justus Lipsius as 'the miracle of our age'. He knew nine languages, was marvellously chaste, refusing, when young, to share the bed of a very illustrious man, was devoted to the Virgin Mary, was feared as much by heretics as Hector by the Greeks or Achilles by the Trojans, and died almost blind with the intensive study which he had devoted to the detection and exposure of witches.[99]

Society, it is clear, approved of Rémy and Boguet, de l'Ancre and del Rio, and they themselves were entirely content with their work. They, after all, were the scholars, the rationalists of the time, while the sceptics were the enemies of reason. Such sceptics were Platonists, Hermetics, Paracelsians – in which case they were witches themselves and deserved to be burnt, as Giordano Bruno and Vanini were – or they were 'Epicureans', 'libertines', 'Pyrrhonists', who distrusted human reason and reduced its finest constructions to a powder of doubt. Such was Montaigne, who, having attended a witch-burning at some petty court in Germany, remarked that 'it is rating our conjectures highly to roast people alive for them'.[100] Against such fancies the guardians of reason and education naturally stood firm, and orthodoxy was protected, impartially, by the miracle of Catholic learning, the Jesuit del Rio, and the Protestant Solomon, King James.

Indeed, the more learned a man was in the traditional scholarship of the time, the more likely he was to support the witch-doctors. The most ferocious of witch-burning princes, we often find, are also the most cultured patrons of contemporary learning. The Catholic Prince-Bishop of Würzburg, Julius Echter von Mespelbrunn, who introduced the craze into his territory in the 1590s, was a universal man of the time, polite, learned and enlightened – with the enlightenment of the Counter-Reformation.[101] His Protestant contemporary, Heinrich Julius, Duke of Brunswick, is described as 'unquestionably the most learned prince of his time' – and he was a contemporary of our James I. He was skilled in mathematics, chemistry, natural science, Latin, Greek and Hebrew. He was a jurist who preferred the Pandects to the Bible and read the Codex rather than a romance; an architect who designed the buildings of his new University of Helmstedt; a poet and a playwright. In his plays he dwelt with unction on the moral duty of princes to burn witches, and throughout his reign (which he began by expelling the Jews from his state) he never failed in that duty. In his lifetime, says a chronicler, the Lechelnholze Square in Wolfenbüttel looked like a little forest, so crowded were the stakes; works of gross superstition were gratefully dedicated to him;[102] and at his death, his court-preacher, enumerating his virtues, dwelt especially on his zeal in burning witches 'according to God's word'.[103]

The European witch-craze of the 1590s, which elicited so many screams of orthodoxy, did at least elicit one protest.

In 1592, eight years after Scot's protest in England, Cornelis Loos, a devout Catholic, ventured to suggest that night-flying and the sabbat were imaginary, that *incubi* and *succubi* did not exist, and that confessions extracted by torture were a means of shedding innocent blood. But Loos, unlike Scot, never reached the public. The Cologne printer to whom he offered his book sensed the danger. Loos was denounced, imprisoned and forced to a humiliating recantation. The good Bishop Binsfeld was present at his recantation and the good Jesuit del Rio published the text of it as a prophylactic 'lest some evil demon should succeed' in printing the views which the benevolent authorities had so far suppressed. In fact the prophylactic was unnecessary. In spite of repeated efforts, which cost him further imprisonment, until death by plague saved him from the stake, Loos's book was never published. It remained locked up for three centuries in the Jesuit college at Trier and his shocking views were known only from his officiously published recantation.[104]

But if the orthodox contrived to suppress the critics, they did not succeed in reducing the witches. After 1604 the campaign abated, at least for a time: the return of peace to Europe no doubt helped, and King James himself, having settled down in England, gradually forgot his Scottish ferocity against witches.[105] In those years the main persecution was once again in the Pyrenees. But the reservoir of fear remained even when it was not in use; those mountain streams continued to feed it; and when religious war returned to Europe the witches were suddenly found, once again, to have increased alarmingly during the years of peace. In the 1620s, with the destruction of Protestantism in Bohemia and the Palatinate, the Catholic reconquest of Germany was resumed. In 1629, with the Edict of Restitution, its basis seemed complete. Those same years saw, in central

Europe at least, the worst of all witch-persecutions, the climax of the European craze.

All over Europe (as a Jesuit historian admits) the witch-trials multiplied with the Catholic reconquest.[106] In some areas the lord or bishop was the instigator, in others the Jesuits. Sometimes local witch-committees were set up to further the work. Among prince-bishops, Philipp Adolf von Ehrenberg of Würzburg was particularly active: in his reign of eight years (1623–31) he burnt 900 persons, including his own nephew, nineteen Catholic priests, and children of seven who were said to have had intercourse with demons.[107] The years 1627–9 were dreadful years in Baden, recently reconquered for Catholicism by Tilly: there were 70 victims in Ortenau, 79 in Offenburg. In Eichstatt, a Bavarian prince-bishopric, a judge claimed the death of 274 witches in 1629. At Reichertsofen an der Paar, in the district of Neuburg, 50 were executed between November 1628 and August 1630. In the three prince-archbishoprics of the Rhineland the fires were also relit. At Coblenz, the seat of the Prince-Archbishop of Trier, 24 witches were burnt in 1629; at Schlettstadt at least 30 – the beginning of a five-year persecution. In Mainz, too, the burnings were renewed. At Cologne the City Fathers had always been merciful, much to the annoyance of the prince-archbishop, but in 1627 he was able to put pressure on the city and it gave in.[108] Naturally enough, the persecution raged most violently in Bonn, his own capital. There the chancellor and his wife and the archbishop's secretary's wife were executed, children of three and four years were accused of having devils for their paramours, and students and small boys of noble birth were sent to the bonfire.[109]

The craze of the 1620s was not confined to Germany: it raged also across the Rhine in Alsace, Lorraine and Franche-Comté. In the lands ruled by the abbey of Luxeuil, in

Franche-Comté, the years 1628–30 have been described as an '*épidémie démoniaque*'. '*Le mal va croissant chaque jour*', declared the magistrates of Dôle, '*et cette malheureuse engeance va pullulant de toutes parts.*' The witches, they said, 'in the hour of death accuse an infinity of others in fifteen or sixteen other villages'.[110]

But the worst persecution of all, in those years, was probably at Bamberg. There the prince-bishop was Johann Georg II Fuchs von Dornheim, known as the *Hexenbischof* or 'witch-bishop'. He built a 'witch-house', complete with torture-chamber adorned with appropriate biblical texts, and in his ten-year reign (1623–33) he is said to have burnt 600 witches. He, too, had his court-prophet, his suffragan, Bishop Forner, who wrote a learned book on the subject.[111] One of their victims was the bishop's chancellor, Dr Haan, burnt as a witch for showing suspicious leniency as a judge. Under torture he confessed to having seen five burgomasters of Bamberg at the sabbat, and they too were duly burnt. One of them, Johannes Julius, under fierce torture confessed that he had renounced God, given himself to the Devil, and seen twenty-seven of his colleagues at the sabbat. But afterwards, from prison, he contrived to smuggle a letter out to his daughter Veronica, giving a full account of his trial. 'Now my dearest child', he concluded, 'you have here all my acts and confessions, for which I must die. It is all falsehood and invention, so help me God. . . . They never cease to torture until one says something. . . . If God sends no means of bringing the truth to light, our whole kindred will be burnt.'[112]

Johannes Julius's *cri de coeur*, which must represent hundreds of unuttered cries from inarticulate victims, found one response. The terrible persecution of the 1620s caused a crisis within the very order which did so much to direct it: the Jesuits. Already, in 1617, Adam Tanner, a Jesuit of

Ingolstadt, had begun to entertain very elementary doubts
which had raised an outcry against him in his order. Now
another Jesuit, Friedrich Spee, was more radically converted
by his experience as a confessor of witches in the great persecution at Würzburg. That experience, which turned his
hair prematurely white, convinced him that all confessions
were worthless, being based solely on torture, and that not a
single witch whom he had led to the stake had been guilty.
Since he could not utter his thoughts otherwise – for, as he
wrote, he dreaded the fate of Tanner – he wrote a book
which he intended to circulate in manuscript, anonymously.
But a friend secretly conveyed it to the Protestant city of
Rinteln and it was there printed in 1631 under the title
Cautio Criminalis.

Spee's work was not the only critical work produced by
the massacres of the 1620s;[113] but it was the most eloquent
protest against the persecution of witches that had yet
appeared. Like Tanner and all the early enemies of the
craze, he did not doubt the reality of witchcraft. But he was
convinced that, although 'all Germany smokes everywhere
with bonfires which obscure the light', he had not yet seen
a real witch, and that 'however much the Princes burn, they
can never burn out the evil'. It was torture, and torture
alone, which caused denunciation and confession. The whole
'science' of the witch-doctors was based on torture. 'All that
Rémy, Binsfield, del Rio and the rest tell us is based on
stories extracted by torture.' Torture proves nothing, nothing
at all. 'Torture fills our Germany with witches and unheard-
of wickedness, and not only Germany but any nation that
attempts it. . . . If all of us have not confessed ourselves
witches, that is only because we have not all been tortured.'
And who, he asked, were the men who demanded these
tortures? Jurists in search of gain, credulous villagers and
'those theologians and prelates who quietly enjoy their

speculations and know nothing of the squalor of prisons, the weight of chains, the implements of torture, the lamentations of the poor – things far beneath their dignity.' We think at once of Nicolas Rémy, writing elegant verses in his fine house at Les Charmes in Lorraine, of Pierre de l'Ancre retiring with his Muses to the grotto of his *cottage orné* on the Garonne, of Fr del Rio in his devout cell, growing blind with study of the Fathers and stiff with prayer to the Virgin.

We might also at this time think of another, and this time a Lutheran scholar. In 1635, four years after the publication of Spee's book, Benedict Carpzov published his great work, *Practica Rerum Criminalium*, dealing with the trial of witches. Carpzov had probably read Spee. He admitted that torture was capable of grave abuse and had led to thousands of false confessions throughout Europe. But he concluded that, *suadente necessitate*, it should still be used, even on those who seemed innocent; and his view of innocence was not liberal. He maintained that even those who merely believed that they had been at the sabbat should be executed, for the belief implied the will. From 'the faithful ministers of the Devil, who bravely defend his kingdom' – i.e. sceptics like Weyer with their 'frivolous' arguments – he appeals to the Catholic authorities: the *Malleus*, Bodin, Rémy, del Rio. And having thus restated the sound doctrine – his book became 'the *Malleus* of Lutheranism' – he would live to a ripe old age and look back on a meritorious life in the course of which he had read the Bible from cover to cover fifty-three times, taken the sacrament every week, greatly intensified the methods and efficacy of torture, and procured the death of 20,000 persons.

Thus Spee, for all his eloquence, achieved no more than Loos or Scot or Weyer before him. His attack, like theirs, was not upon the belief in witches – indeed, he was less radical than Weyer, who, though the earliest, was the boldest

of them all. By his personal influence he may have reduced
the savagery of the persecution in the next generation, for
the most enlightened of seventeenth-century prince-bishops
of Würzburg, Johann Philipp von Schönborn, Elector of
Mainz, the friend and patron of Leibniz, was convinced by
him and worked to undo the damage wrought by his predecessors.[114] But if the witch-craze of the 1620s died down in
the 1630s that was largely due to extraneous causes : war and
foreign domination. The French in Lorraine and Franche-
Comté, the Swedes in Mecklenburg, Franconia and Bavaria,
put a stop to this social war among the natives, just as the
English, in the 1650s, would do in Scotland. They did so
not necessarily because they were more liberal – the spectacular French witch-trial of Urbain Grandier took place in
the 1630s, Matthew Hopkins would have a free hand in
England in the 1640s, and the witch-craze would break
out in Sweden in the 1660s – but simply because they
were foreign, and witch-trials were essentially a social, internal matter. And anyway, the stop was not permanent.
Once the hand of the foreigner was removed, the natives
would return to their old ways. As in Scotland, relieved of
English occupation in the 1660s, so in Mecklenburg after
the withdrawal of the Swedes, so in Lorraine after the depar-
ture of the French, the old persecution would break out
again. Indeed, in some areas the persecution was worse at
the end of the seventeenth than at the end of the sixteenth
century. In 1591 the Rostock professor of law, J. G. Gödelmann, had urged liberalism and clemency on the Mecklenburg judges. A century later his successor Johann Klein
asserted in print the reality of *succubi* and *incubi* and demanded (and secured) death by burning for those who were
accused of intercourse with them, and his arguments were
supported in print by the dean of the faculty of theology at
Rostock thirty years later. As late as 1738 the dean of the

faculty of law at Rostock demanded that witches be extirpated by 'fire and sword' and boasted of the number of
stakes he had seen 'on one hill'.[115]

Thus the intellectual basis of the witch-craze remained
firm all through the seventeenth century. No critic had improved on the arguments of Weyer; none had attacked the
substance of the myth; all that successive sceptics had done
was to cast doubt on its practical interpretation: to question
the value of confessions, the efficacy of torture, the identification of particular witches. The myth itself remained untouched, at least in appearance. Artificial though it was,
recent though it was, it had become part of the structure of
thought, and time had so entwined it with other beliefs, and
indeed with social interests, that it seemed impossible to
destroy it. In happy times men might forget it, at least in
practice. In the early sixteenth century there had seemed a
good chance that it might be forgotten – that is, dissolve
again into scattered peasant superstitions. But those happy
times had not lasted. The ideological struggle of Reformation
and Counter-Reformation – that grim struggle which was
so disastrous in European intellectual history – had revived
the dying witch-craze just as it had revived so many other
obsolescent habits of thought: biblical fundamentalism,
theological history, scholastic Aristoteleanism. All these had
seemed in retreat in the age of Erasmus and Machiavelli
and Ficino; all returned a generation later to block the progress of thought for another century.

Every crucial stage in the ideological struggle of the
Reformation was a stage also in the revival and perpetuation
of the witch-craze. In the 1480s the Dominicans had made
war, as they thought, on the relics of medieval heresy. That
was the time of the Witch Bull and the *Malleus*, and the
renewed persecution in those 'Alpine valleys cold' in which
del Rio would afterwards see the eternal source of witch-

craft and Milton the ancient cradle of Protestantism. In the 1560s the Protestant missionaries had set out to evangelize the countries of northern Europe whose rulers had accepted the new faith, and at once the witch-hunt had been renewed by them. From 1580 the Catholic Counter-Reformation had begun to reconquer northern Europe and the persecution became, once again, a Catholic terror, with the new Jesuits replacing the old Dominicans as evangelists. It was then that the Spaniard Francisco Peña, a canon lawyer in the Roman Curia, collected and summarized the conclusions of the Roman Inquisitors: for no subject, he wrote, was now more frequently discussed by the Catholic clergy than sorcery and divination.[116] Finally, the Thirty Years War, the last stage of the ideological struggle, brings with it the worst persecution of all: the '*épidémie démoniaque*' which reached its climax in the year of Catholic restoration, 1629.

Admittedly there are exceptions to this general rule. In England, for instance, the persecution of witches was always trivial by continental standards* and its closest student has

* The figures commonly given for the execution of witches in England are grotesquely exaggerated. Lea himself, in his *History of the Inquisition in Spain*, IV, 247, estimated the number of victims in Britain as 90,000, 'of whom about a fourth may be credited to Scotland'. But Mr C. L. Ewen's careful study of the records of the Home Circuit has discredited all such wild guesses. He concludes that between 1542 and 1736 'less than one thousand' persons were executed for witchcraft in England (*Witch Hunting and Witch Trials*, 1929, p. 112). The executions in Scotland, where torture was used, were not less but far more numerous: probably 4400 in the ninety years from 1590 to 1680 (see G. F. Black, in 'A Calendar of Witchcraft Cases in Scotland 1510–1727', *Bulletin of New York Public Library*, XLI, no. 11 (November 1937), p. 823). In fact, allowing a very modest figure for the remaining 83 years of the witch-laws in Scotland (they lasted from 1563 to 1736), and reckoning the population of Scotland as equivalent to one-fifth of that of England, we may say that the density of execution was twenty-five times as great in Scotland as in England.

been able to detect no pattern in it. 'There was in fact', writes Ewen, 'no clearly defined periodic wave of witch-mania sweeping through the country, but rather a succession of sporadic outbreaks. The underlying current of superstition, always present, manifested itself unpleasantly whenever and wherever fanaticism was unusually rampant, the influence of one man being sufficient to raise the excess of zeal to the danger point.'[117] Perhaps this may safely be said of England, where persecution, thanks to the absence of judicial torture, never became a craze. But does not such an answer, even there, beg the question? For why was fanaticism, at some times, 'unusually rampant'? Why did 'one man', like Matthew Hopkins, appear in 1645 rather than in 1635? In fact, when we compare England with the Continent, we see that the rhythm of English persecution follows very closely that of the continental craze of which it is a pale reflection. On the Continent, the great persecutions are after 1560, when the Protestant evangelists carry it northwards; after 1580 as the Counter-Reformation overtakes them, and especially in the 1590s, those years of general economic depression and European plague; and in the 1620s, during the Catholic reconquest of the Thirty Years War. In England persecution similarly begins in the 1560s with the return of the Marian exiles; it similarly takes new life in the 1580s and 1590s, the years of Catholic plots, war and fear; and thereafter, if its course is different – if it virtually ceases for the duration of the Thirty Years War – this very divergence is perhaps the exception which proves the rule. For England – to her shame, cried the Puritans – was uninvolved in the Thirty Years War. In the 1640s, when civil and ideological war came to England, witches were persecuted in England too.*

* The trials of witches in England fell off markedly after 1617, when James I, in Fuller's words, 'receding from what he had

Another exception which may yet prove the general rule is supplied by Sweden. The Swedish Lutheran Church, like the Anglican Church, was neither a persecuting nor a proselytizing body, at least in its first century. When it came in contact with the Lapps of the north, it found – as the Roman Church had found in the Pyrenees and the Alps – a different society, racially as well as socially different, half-pagan in religion, given over, it seemed, in that Arctic cold, to bizarre witch-beliefs.[118] But as it did not seek to assimilate these harmless dissenters their beliefs were not persecuted, and the Lapland witches remained always outside the general European witch-craze. In 1608 Sweden, like other Lutheran countries, adopted the Mosaic penalties for offences previously punished by the Church courts; but even this provision, which was used to justify witch-burning elsewhere, had no such consequence in Sweden. There witch-trials remained sporadic and episodic, and no great native witch-doctor, like King James in Scotland, or Perkins in

---

written in his *Demonologie*, grew first diffident of, and then flatly to deny, the workings of witches and devils, as but falsehoods and delusions'. (Notestein, *A History of Witchcraft in England*, pp. 142-4; Ewen, *Witch Hunting and Witch Trials*, pp. 98 ff.; but see also G. L. Burr's review of Ewen in *American Historical Review*, xxxv, 1929–30, pp. 844 ff.) Under the personal rule of Charles I executions for witchcraft ceased altogether in England, at least in the counties of the Home Circuit (Ewen, op. cit.), and were at least severely cut down in Scotland: one of the articles of complaint against the Scottish bishops in 1638 was for 'staying' such proceedings (W. L. Mathieson, *Politics and Religion. A Study in Scottish History from the Reformation to the Revolution* (Glasgow, 1902, II, 157–9). However, the events of 1640 changed all that in both countries. In Scotland the General Assembly of 1640, having got rid of the bishops, required all ministers to nose out witches and urge the enforcement of the law against them (ibid., p. 159), which they did, to some tune, and in England more witches were executed in 1645 than in any year before or since (see the statistics in Ewen, op. cit., pp. 102–8, 221–31).

England, or Hemmingsen in Denmark, or Gödelmann in Mecklenburg, sought to erect in Sweden the full-blown demonology of Europe. Indeed, as we have seen, in the Thirty Years War the Swedish generals, obeying explicit orders from Queen Christina, suppressed the witch-fires in Germany. It was not till the 1660s that a change came to Sweden, and then it was in circumstances which recall the European outbreaks.

For in the 1660s the established Lutheran Church in Sweden became intolerant. Like the established Calvinist Church in Scotland, it had shaken itself free from alliance with other, more liberal Protestant parties, and its Puritan leaders prepared to advertise their purity by a great witch-hunt. In 1664 it branded as heretical the Syncretist movement – the movement of pan-Protestantism which had been so useful in the Thirty Years War. In 1667 it put out a new declaration of orthodoxy, 'the most rigorous of the century', against the subtle menace of Cartesianism: that Cartesianism which Descartes himself had brought to the Court of Queen Christina. Now that Queen Christina was an exile in Rome, the frightened Church of Sweden resolved to assert itself; its preachers became zealots of their faith, eager to sniff out and condemn heresy; and in the same year the witch-mania was fired by panic fears in the province of Dalårna. 'It is something more than an accident', writes Hr Sundborg, 'that the victory of orthodoxy in 1664 was followed so closely by the outbreak of the persecutions.'[119] The same might be said of all the previous European crazes.

Why did social struggle, in those two centuries, invariably revive this bizarre mythology? We might as well ask, why has economic depression in Germany, from the Middle Ages until this century, so often revived the bizarre mythology of antisemitism: the fables of poisoned wells and ritual murder which were spread at the time of the Crusades, during the

Black Death, in the Thirty Years War, and in the pages of Julius Streicher's Nazi broadsheet, *Der Stürmer*? The question is obviously not simple. It carries us beyond and below the realm of mere intellectual problems. We have here to deal with a mythology which is more than a mere fantasy. It is a social stereotype: a stereotype of fear.

Any society is liable, at times, to collective emotion. There is the exalted 'messianism' which is common in rural societies in medieval Europe; in southern Italy, Spain and Portugal in early modern times; in modern Brazil. There is also the undefined 'great fear', such as ran through rural France at the beginning of the revolution of 1789. And these emotions tend to take stereotyped form. How such stereotypes are built up is a problem in itself; but once they are built up, they can last for generations, even centuries. The stereotype in German society has long been the Jewish conspiracy. In England, from the days of the Spanish Armada till the days of the 'Papal Aggression' of 1851 and the 'Vaticanism' of 1870, it has been the Popish Plot.* In America today it seems to be the Red scare. In continental Europe, in the two centuries after the Witch Bull, it was the witch-craze. So firmly had the mythology of Satan's kingdom been established in the declining Middle Ages that in the first centuries of 'modern' Europe – to use a conventional notation of time – it became the standard form in which the otherwise undefined fears of society became crystallized. Just as psycopathic individuals in those years centred their separate fantasies (or, as the seventeenth-

* Apart from the Gunpowder Plot of 1605 and the Popish Plot of 1678, there was the imaginary Popish Plot reported by Andreas ab Habernfeld in 1640, belief in which was kept alive for many years afterwards; the Irish Massacre of 1641 which still curdled the blood of John Wesley in the next century; the *canard* that it was the Papists who had burnt London in 1666; the myth of the Warmingpan in 1688; the Gordon Riots of 1780, etc. etc.

century doctors would say, their 'melancholy') on the Devil,
and thus gave an apparent objective identity to their subjective experiences, so societies in fear articulated their collective
neuroses about the same obsessive figure, and found a
scapegoat for their fears in his agents, the witches. Both the
individual and the society made this identification because
the Devil, his kingdom and his agents had been made real to
them by the folk-lore of their times; but both, by this identification, sustained and confirmed the same centralizing
folk-lore for their successors.

Thus the mythology created its own evidence, and effective
disproof became ever more difficult. In times of prosperity
the whole subject might be ignored except on a village level,
but in times of fear men do not think clearly : they retreat
to fixed positions, fixed prejudices. So social struggle, political conspiracy, conventual hysteria, private hallucination
were all interpreted in the light of a mythology which, by
now, had been extended to interpret them all, and the craze
was renewed. At each renewal, some bold and humane dis-
senter would seek to challenge the collective hysteria and
cruelty. Ponzinibio would challenge the Dominican inquisitors, Weyer the Protestant persecutors of the 1560s,
Loos and Scot the Catholic and Protestant persecutors of the
1590s, Spee the Catholic torturers of the 1620s and 1630s.
But none of these would do more than question the esoteric
details of the myth and the identification of the victims.
The basis of the myth was beyond their reach. They might
convince educated princes, as Weyer convinced the Duke of
Cleves and Spee the future Prince-Bishop of Würzburg and
Elector of Mainz; and no one should underestimate the influence that a prince might have to extend or suppress the
effect of the craze.[120] But their opponents appealed against
them to a lower level – to petty magistrates and clerical
tribunes [121] – and on that lower level kept the craze alive. It

remained alive until the eighteenth-century Enlightenment, defended by clergymen, lawyers and scholars, and capable of being reanimated by any sudden coincidence of forces, when politicians or judges surrendered to social fear. The great outbreaks in Sweden in 1668–77, in Salzburg in 1677–81, in Mecklenburg after 1690, and in colonial New England in 1692 show that if the Thirty Years War was the last occasion of international mania, national mania could still be aroused. The fire still lurked beneath the cinders.

Nevertheless, after the Thirty Years War something had happened. It was not merely that the war was over. The stereotype itself had weakened. In Protestant and Catholic countries alike the myth had lost its force. In the 1650s Cyrano de Bergerac could write in France as if it were already dead, at least among educated men.[122] Twenty years later, in 1672, the law would recognize its death when Colbert abolished the charge of *sorcellerie sabbatique*. In Cromwellian England the 1650s saw an outbreak of books repudiating witch-trials; the frequent discovery and execution of witches, Francis Osborne told his son in 1656, 'makes me think the strongest fascination is encircled within the ignorance of the judges, malice of the witnesses, or stupidity of the poor parties accused'.[123] In Calvinist Geneva, once so ferocious, the last witch was burnt in 1652: the urban aristocracy had by now reduced the clergy to order. At the same time the magistrates of Bern issued an ordinance to restrain the witch-judges. In 1657 even the Church of Rome, which had put all critical books on the Index, issued 'a tardy *instructio* urging her inquisitors to circumspection'.[124] From now on, in spite of local recrudescence and intellectual support, the climate of opinion has changed, and the assertors of witchcraft, but recently so confident, find themselves on the defensive. While the social stereotypes of the Jew in Germany and the Popish Plot in England retain their plausibility, that of the witch is failing, and we have to ask, how did this happen? Why did a mythology which, against all likelihood, had been prolonged for two centuries, suddenly lose its force? For although the old laws may remain on the statute book and the old beliefs will linger in school and cloister, the systematic mythology, and the social force which it inspired, are crumbling. By 1700 the 'craze' is over: the infidels, as John Wesley was to lament, 'have hooted witchcraft out of the world'.

5
DECLINE

THE decline and apparently final collapse of the witch-craze in the late seventeenth century, while other such social stereotypes retained their power, is a revolution which is surprisingly difficult to document. We see the controversies continue. Important names appear on both sides – but the greater names, at least in England, are on the side of the craze, not against it. How can the obscure and tipsy Oxford scholar John Wagstaffe or the crotchety Yorkshire surgeon–parson John Webster compete with the names of Sir Thomas Browne and Richard Baxter and the Cambridge Platonists Ralph Cudworth, Henry More and Joseph Glanville? And yet on neither side are the arguments new: they are the arguments which have always been used. On the side of orthodoxy some caution can be observed: the grosser and more preposterous details of the demonologists are silently dropped (although Continental and Scottish lawyers and clergy continued to assert them) and the argument is given a more philosophic base. But on the sceptical side there is no advance. Webster is no more modern than Weyer. Nevertheless, without new argument on either side the intellectual belief quietly dissolved. The witch-trials, in spite of a few last outbursts, came to an end. The witch-laws were re-pealed, almost without debate.

It has been pointed out that, in this reform, Protestant countries led the way. England and Holland were regarded, in 1700, as countries long since emancipated while the Catholic prince-bishops of Germany were still burning away. Inside Germany, says a German scholar, the Protes-

tant states abandoned persecution a full generation before the
Catholic.[125] In mixed societies, like Alsace, the Catholic lords
had always been fiercer than the Protestant.[126] And certainly
Catholic manuals continued to insist on demonological doc-
trine when the Protestant writers had conveniently forgotten
it. However, in view of the undoubted part played by the
Protestant Churches in forwarding the craze after 1560, we
should perhaps be chary of claiming any special virtue for
Protestantism in resisting it after 1650. Calvinist and
Lutheran doctrines were as uncompromising, Calvinist and
Lutheran clergy as ferocious as Catholic; and where the
Calvinist or Lutheran clergy had effective power – as in
Scotland or Mecklenburg – the craze continued as long as in
any Catholic country. To the very end, honours remained
even between the two religions. If the last witch-burning in
Europe was in Catholic Poland in 1793, that was an illegal
act : witch-trials had been abolished in Poland in 1787. The
last legal execution was in Protestant Glarus, in Switzerland,
in 1782. Appropriately the craze which had been born in the
Alps retreated thither to die.

But if the power of the clergy, Protestant or Catholic, prolonged the craze, their weakness hastened its end; and the
clergy were undoubtedly weaker in some Protestant than in
most Catholic countries. This was particularly true in the
United Netherlands. The Dutch Calvinist clergy, the *Predi-
kants*, were notoriously intolerant; but unlike their Scottish
brethren, they were never allowed to exercise or influence
jurisdiction. This was discovered even during the national
revolution. In 1581 Lambert Daneau, the most important
Huguenot preacher after his masters Calvin and Beza, and
incidentally, like them, a formidable witch-hunter, received
a call to a chair in the new University of Leiden. He
answered the call. But he had not been long in Leiden before
his theocratic pretensions brought him into trouble. The

Council of Leiden, he was told, would resist the Inquisition of Geneva no less than that of Spain; and he found it prudent to leave the Netherlands to rule over a more submissive flock in Pyrenean France.[127] In the next century the Dutch Calvinist clergy continued to demand death for witchcraft. Their intellectual oracles, Junius, Rivetus, Voëtius, were unambiguous on this point.[128] The greatest and latest of them was Voëtius, professor and rector of the University of Utrecht. He denounced, with equal assurance, the theories of Galileo, Harvey and Descartes and marshalled a series of massive arguments to show that there are witches and that they should not be suffered to live. It particularly infuriated him that Scot's work, though rightly burnt in England, had been translated into Dutch and had corrupted many readers in the republic, already only too full of 'libertines' and 'semi-libertines'.[129] He was no doubt thinking of 'Arminians' like Hugo Grotius, who would put authority in matters of religion in the hands of lay magistrates and declared that the Mosaic penalties were no longer binding; or Episcopius, who denied the reality of the witch's pact with Satan, the very basis of witchcraft; or Johann Greve, who, like Weyer, came from Cleves and urged the abolition of torture in witch-trials.[130] It was an Arminian too, 'the Arminian printer' Thomas Basson, the printer of Grotius and Arminius himself, who had translated Scot's book and published it in Leiden; and it was the Arminian historian Pieter Schrijver, or Scriberius, who had set him on.[131] The Calvinist clergy succeeded in condemning Arminianism, procured the exile of Grotius and hounded Greve from his parish at Arnhem. But they were never able to capture criminal jurisdiction from the lay magistrates, and it was clearly for this reason, not because of any virtue in their doctrine, that no witch was burnt in Holland after 1597, and that witchcraft trials ceased in 1610.[132]

Was the collapse of the witch-craze then due merely to the victory of the laity over the clergy: a victory that was more easily won in Protestant countries, where the clergy had already been weakened, than in Catholic countries where it had retained its power? The inference is natural, and no doubt partly true: but it can only be partly true. For whence did the laity acquire their ideas? The witch-craze may have been first formulated by the clergy, but by 1600 it was being perpetuated by the lawyers. Bodin, Boguet, de l'Ancre, Carpzov were lay magistrates, not clergymen. We have seen the lay magistrates of Lemgo, in Westphalia, imposing the new cold-water test,[81] and those of Dôle, in Franche-Comté, demanding fiercer penalties for the growing pest of witch-craft. It was the lay magistrates of Essex, under the chairmanship of the Puritan Earl of Warwick, who in 1645 condemned a record number of witches to death at Chelmsford assizes, and it was the lay magistrates of Rouen who protested against Colbert's order suspending witch-trials. When we compare these laymen with clergy like the Arminian Greve or the Jesuit Spee, or the Anglican bishops of James I and Charles I, or the Gallican bishops of Richelieu and Mazarin,[133] we have to admit that there are laity and laity, clergy and clergy. No doubt the independent laity of mercantile cities or great courts have a more liberal outlook than the legal caste of provincial towns or petty principalities. But is not the same true of the clergy? Ultimately, the difference is a difference of ideas. The independent laity — educated merchants, officials, gentry — may be freer to receive new ideas than clergy or lawyers; they may give social content and social force to such ideas; but the ideas themselves, as often as not, are generated among the clergy. The Reformation itself, that great social revolution, began as 'une querelle de moines'.

We can see the resistance of the laity to the witch-craze all through its course. It was a resistance to which every witch-doctor paid indignant tribute. But it was a limited resistance: a resistance of scepticism, of common sense, not of positive disbelief or opposite belief. Men revolted against the cruelty of torture, against the implausibility of confessions, against the identification of witches. They did not revolt against the central doctrine of the kingdom of Satan and its war on humanity by means of demons and witches. They had no substitute for such a doctrine. And because that doctrine was established, even accepted, it had provided the central pillar around which other doctrines, other experiences had entwined themselves, adding to its strength. Sceptics might doubt. They might even protest. But neither doubt nor protest was enough. In fair weather the luxury of scepticism might be allowed; but when the storm returned, men fell back again on the old faith, the old orthodoxy.

If the witch-craze were to be attacked at its centre, not merely doubted at its periphery, it was clearly necessary to challenge the whole conception of the kingdom of Satan. This neither Weyer nor Scot nor Spee had done. All through the sixteenth and seventeenth centuries it had been an axiom of faith that the Church was engaged in a life-and-death struggle with Satan. The writers of the *Malleus* had referred, in lamentable tones, to the impending end of the world whose disasters were everywhere visible,[134] and the Protestant writers, reactionary in this as in all else, had used, and intensified, the same language. In the early seventeenth century millennarian ideas, forgotten since the Middle Ages, were revived, and the greatest discovery of a scientific century was declared to be the solution, by a future Fellow of the Royal Society, of the hitherto elusive number of the Beast.[135] But at the very end of the century one writer did attempt to challenge the whole idea of Satan's kingdom. This was the Dutch minister Balthasar Bekker, who in 1690 published the first version of the first volume of his *De Betoverde Weereld*, 'The Enchanted World'.

Both at the time and since Bekker was regarded as the most dangerous enemy of witch-beliefs. The orthodox denounced him in unmeasured tones. Like Greve, seventy years before, he was persecuted by the Calvinist clergy of Holland and ultimately, though protected by the city of Amsterdam, driven out of the ministry. The first two volumes of his book, it is said, sold 4000 copies in two months, and it was translated into French, German and English. Pamphlets were poured out against him. He was held responsible for the cessation of witch-burnings in England and Holland[136] – although witches had never been burnt in England and burnings had long ceased in Holland. Bekker, it has been regularly said, struck at the heart of the witch-craze by destroying belief in the Devil.[137]

Perhaps he did in theory; but did he in fact? When we look closer, we find reasons for doubt. Bekker's foreign reputation seems largely a myth. The controversy over his work was conducted almost entirely in the Dutch language.[138] And that controversy was evidently soon over. In 1696 a Frenchman declared that Bekker's disciples were already falling away, disappointed by his later volumes; and this opinion is confirmed by the fact that the English translation never got beyond the first volume.[139] An Englishman who wished to refute Bekker a few years later, and who sent to Holland 'for all that was writ against him and any replies he had made', could obtain only one small volume in French.[140] The German translation was declared by a good judge to be worthless: the translator, it was said, understood neither Dutch nor German nor his author.[141] By 1706 Bekker seemed forgotten. His work had enjoyed a *succès de scandale* only. And anyway, he had not repudiated belief in the Devil. He merely believed that the Devil, on his fall from Heaven, had been locked up in Hell, unable further to interfere in human affairs. This purely theological point was not likely to cause a revolution in thought. In his particular arguments about witches Bekker was inspired, as he admitted, by Scot, and did not go beyond Scot.

Moreover, Bekker's radicalism was disowned by later, and perhaps more effective, opponents of the witch-craze. If any group of men destroyed the craze in Lutheran Germany it was the Pietists of the University of Halle whose leader, in this respect, was Christian Thomasius, the advocate of the vernacular language. In a series of works, beginning with a university thesis in 1701, Thomasius denounced the folly and cruelty of witch-trials. But he was careful to dissociate himself from Bekker. There is a Devil, Thomasius protests, and there are witches: this 'cannot be denied without great presumption and thoughtlessness'. But Weyer and Scot and Spee have shown that the witches who are tried in Germany are quite different from those witches whose death is prescribed in the Bible, that the demonology of the Church is a mixture of pagan and Jewish superstition, and that confessions produced by torture are false. Again and again Thomasius protests that he is falsely accused of disbelieving in the Devil. He believes in the Devil, he says, and that he still operates, externally and invisibly: he only disbelieves that the Devil has horns and a tail; and he believes in witches: he only disbelieves in their pact with the Devil, the sabbat, *incubi* and *succubi*. When we examine his arguments we find that neither he nor his friends at Halle went beyond Scot or Spee or those English writers, Wagstaffe and Webster, whose works they caused to be translated into German.[142] And yet it is equally clear that the arguments which had been advanced in vain by Scot and Spee were effective when advanced by Thomasius. The witch-craze did not collapse because Bekker dislodged the Devil from his central position: the Devil decayed quietly with the witch-belief;[143] and why the witch-belief decayed – why the critical arguments which were regarded as unplausible in 1563 and in 1594 and in 1631 were found plausible in 1700 – is mysterious still.

The nineteenth-century liberal historians did indeed offer an answer. They saw the controversy as a straight contest between superstition and reason, between theology and science, between the Church and 'rationalism'. The Englishman Lecky, the Americans White, Lea and Burr, the German Hansen, write as if the irrationality of the witch-beliefs had always been apparent to the natural reason of man and as if the prevalence of such beliefs could be explained only by clerical bigotry allied with political power. This bigotry, they seem to say, was artificially created. The persecution began, says Burr, because the Inquisition, having fulfilled its original purpose of destroying the Albigensian heretics, found itself with nothing to do and so 'turned its idle hands to the extirpation of witches'.[144] From that time onwards, these writers suggest, the 'rationalists' fought a long battle against clerical and conservative bigotry. At first it was a losing battle, but at last persistence brought its reward: the tide turned and the battle was ultimately won. And yet, these writers seem to be saying, even now it is not quite won. As long as there is religion, there is a danger of superstition, and superstition will break out in these and such forms. The world – so Hansen ended his great work – will not be free till the still undefeated residue of superstition has been expelled from the religious systems of the modern world.

Today such a distinction between 'reason' and 'superstition' is difficult to maintain. We have seen the darkest forms of superstitious belief and superstitious cruelty springing again not out of half-purged religious systems, but out of new, purely secular roots. We have seen that social stereotypes are more lasting than religious systems – indeed, that religious systems may be only temporary manifestations of a more deep-seated social attitude. We have also come to distrust too rational explanations. The picture of the Inquisition using up its idle machinery against witches simply to prevent it from rusting cannot convince us. Finally, we can no longer see intellectual history as a direct contest between reason and faith, reason and superstition. We recognize that even rationalism is relative: that it operates within a general philosophic context, and that it cannot properly be detached from this context.

The liberal historians of the nineteenth century supposed that it could be so detached: that those men who, in the sixteenth and seventeenth centuries, were revolted by the cruelty of witch-trials, or rejected the absurdities of witch-beliefs, ought to have seen that it was not enough to protest against these incidental excesses: they should have seen that the whole system had no rational basis. In their impatience with the critics of the past, these liberal historians sometimes seem to us absurdly anachronistic. When he examines the work of Weyer, Lea becomes positively snappish. Why, he asks, is Weyer so 'illogical'? Why cannot he see 'the fatal defect' in his own reasoning? Weyer, he exclaims, was 'as credulous as any of his contemporaries': his work is an extraordinary mixture of 'common sense' and 'folly'; 'nothing can exceed the ingenious perversity' of his views, his belief in magic and demons while he rejects the sabbat and *succubi*. No wonder 'his labours had so limited a result'.[145] It is clear that, to Lea, 'reason', 'logic', is a self-contained, independent system of permanent validity. What is obvious in nineteenth-century Philadelphia must have been equally obvious in sixteenth-century Germany. We are reminded of Macaulay's remark that 'a Christian of the fifth century with a Bible is neither better nor worse situated than a Christian of the nineteenth century with a Bible' and that the absurdity of a literal interpretation was 'as great and as obvious in the sixteenth century as it is now'.[146]

But the difficulty of the men of the sixteenth and seventeenth centuries was that witch-beliefs were not detachable from their general context. The mythology of the Dominicans was an extension, with the aid of peasant superstition, feminine hysteria and clerical imagination, of a whole cosmology. It was also rooted in permanent social attitudes. In order to dismantle this grotesque mental construction, it was not enough – it was not possible – to look at its component ideas in isolation. They could not be so isolated, nor was there yet an independent 'reason' detached from the context of which they too were a part. If men were to revise their views on witchcraft, the whole context of those views had to be revised. Then, and then only, this extension – the weakest part of it, but theoretically essential to it – would dissolve. Until that had happened, all that men could do was to doubt its more questionable details. Even then, even when that had happened, the repudiation would not be complete: for it would be merely intellectual. Unless there were also a social transformation, the social basis of the belief would remain – although a new stereotype would have to be devised in order to express the hostility which it had embodied.

How inseparable the witch-beliefs were from the whole philosophy of the time is clear when we look at the demonologists as a class, and at their whole intellectual output, not merely at their treatises on witches and witchcraft. Some of them, of course, are specialists, like Boguet, or are concerned, as lawyers, with witchcraft as an object of the criminal law. But the majority of them are philosophers in a wider field. To St Thomas Aquinas, the greatest of medieval Dominicans, as to Francisco de Vitoria, the greatest of Spanish Renaissance Dominicans,[147] demonology is but one aspect of the world which they seek to understand.

Scribonius, who defended the cold-water test, was a professor of philosophy who wrote on natural science and mathematics. The Zwinglian Erastus was a physician, a theologian, a political philosopher as well as a writer on witches. The Lutheran Hyperius, the great doctor of Marburg whose authority as a demonologist was cited by King James, was an Aristotelean humanist who had studied at a dozen different universities and wrote on as many different subjects.[148] The Lutheran Heinrich Nicolai, professor of philosophy at Danzig in the mid seventeenth century, wrote on 'the whole of human knowledge' before coming to the specialized department of witchcraft.[149] The Calvinists Daneau and Perkins and Voëtius were the encyclopedists of their party in France, England and Holland: Daneau wrote on Christian physics and Christian politics as well as on witches and every other subject; Perkins was an oracle on all moral questions; Voëtius, like Bacon, took all learning for his province – only, unlike Bacon, in every direction, he resisted its advancement. Bodin was the universal genius of his age. King James and del Rio were men of multifarious, if conservative learning. When we look at the work of these men as a whole, we see that they wrote upon demonology not necessarily because they had a special interest in it, but because they had to do so. Men who sought to express a consistent philosophy of nature could not exclude what was a necessary and logical, if unedifying extension of it. They would not have agreed with the modern historian of magic that 'these off-scourings of the criminal courts and torture-chamber, of popular gossip and local scandal, are certainly beneath the dignity of our investigation'.[150] Rather, they would have agreed with Bertrand Russell that to flinch from such necessary consequences of their professed beliefs, merely because they were disagreeable or absurd, would be a sign of 'the intellectual enfeeblement of orthodoxy'.

Equally, those who questioned witch-beliefs could not reject them in isolation. Pomponazzi, Agrippa, Cardano are universal philosophers, Weyer and Ewich medical men with a general philosophy of Nature. If they reject witch-beliefs, it is because they are prepared to question the accepted philosophy of the natural world, of which witch-beliefs were an extension, and to envisage a completely different system. But few men, in the sixteenth century, were prepared to make that effort. Failing such an effort, there were only two ways in which a man could express his dissent from the orthodox demonologists. He could accept the basic philosophical orthodoxy of his time and confine his criticism to the validity of particular methods or particular interpretations. This was the way of Scot and Spee, who believed in witches, but not in the modern methods of identifying them. Or he could recognize that the science of demonology rested firmly on human reason, but doubt the infallibility of such reason and so reserve a liberty of 'Pyrrhonist' scepticism. This was the way of Montaigne, who dared to refer to the unanswerable conclusions of scholastic reason as 'conjectures'.

Neither of these methods was radical enough, by itself, to destroy the intellectual belief in witches. The criticism of a Scot or a Spee might be acceptable in fair times, but it did not touch the basis of belief and with the return of a 'great fear' it would soon be forgotten. The scepticism of a Montaigne might undermine orthodoxy, but it could equally sustain it – as it often did – by undermining heresy. Montaigne himself was claimed as an ally by his witch-burning friend de l'Ancre.[151] The greatest of French sceptics, Pierre Bayle, left the witch-craze exactly where he found it, and his English contemporary, Joseph Glanville, used scepticism positively to reinforce belief in witchcraft.[152] What ultimately destroyed the witch-craze, on an intellectual level, was not the two-edged arguments of the sceptics, nor was it modern 'rationalism', which could exist only within a new context of thought. It was not even the arguments of Bekker, tied as they were to biblical fundamentalism. It was the new philosophy, a philosophical revolution which changed the whole concept of Nature and its operations. That revolution did not occur within the narrow field of demonology, and therefore we cannot usefully trace it by a study which is confined to that field. It occurred in a far wider field, and the men who made it did not launch their attack on so marginal an area of Nature as demonology. Demonology, after all, was but an appendix of medieval thought, a later refinement of scholastic philosophy. The attack was directed at the centre; and when it had prevailed at the centre, there was no need to struggle for the outworks: they had been turned.

This, it seems to me, is the explanation of the apparent silence of the great thinkers of the early seventeenth century, the philosophers of natural science, natural law, secular history. Why, we are asked, did Bacon, Grotius, Selden not express disbelief in witchcraft? Their silence, or their incidental concessions to orthodoxy, have even been taken, by some, to argue belief. But this, I suggest, is a wrong inference. The writers who make it are, once again, treating the subject in isolation. If we wish to interpret reticence, the correct method is not to examine, with rabbinical exactitude, particular breaches of reticence, but first to consider the whole context of a man's thought. When we do that, the explanation, I believe, becomes clear. Bacon, Grotius, Selden may have been reticent on witches. So, for that matter, was Descartes. Why should they court trouble on a secondary, peripheral issue? On the central issue they were not reticent, and it is in their central philosophy that we must see the battle that they were fighting: a battle which would cause the world of witches, ultimately, to wither away.[153]

Nevertheless, what a struggle it had been for the centre!

No mere scepticism, no mere 'rationalism', could have driven out the old cosmology. A rival faith had been needed, and it therefore seems a little unfair in Lea to blame the earliest and greatest opponent of the craze for being hardly less 'credulous' than his adversaries.[154] The first rival faith had been Renaissance Platonism, 'natural magic': a faith which filled the universe with 'demons', but at the same time subjected them to a harmonious Nature whose machinery they served and whose laws they operated. Ultimately, Renaissance Platonism had been left with its demons, and the Cambridge Platonists, insulated in their fenland cloister, were to provide some of the last intellectual defenders of witch-beliefs.* But the impulse which it had given was continued by other philosophers: by Bacon with his 'purified magic', by Descartes with his universal, 'mechanical' laws of Nature, in which demons were unnecessary. It was Descartes, Thomasius and his friends agreed, who dealt the final blow to the witch-craze in western Europe [155] – which perhaps explains, better than the original Protestantism of Colbert, the early suspension of witch-trials in France. Queen Christina of Sweden, who ordered the witch-trials to cease in the Swedish-occupied parts of Germany, † had herself been

* The Cambridge Platonists adopted neo-Platonic ideas just at the time when Platonism, from a liberating, was turning into a reactionary force. But Cambridge itself was in many ways cut off from the Baconian and Cartesian ideas which were accepted in Oxford in the 1650s. Even Newton was in many ways imprisoned in the backward-looking Puritan theology of Restoration Cambridge.

† Her order, of February 1649–50, is printed in Hauber, *Bibliotheca ... Magica*, III, 250. It is a remarkably enlightened document. The Queen states that the spread of witch-trials is of dangerous consequence, past experience showing that the longer they are allowed to continue, the deeper men are involved 'in an inextricable labyrinth'. She therefore orders the immediate cessation of all such inquisitions and trials and restitution *ad integrum* to all persons held on such charges.

the pupil of Descartes. Gustaf Rosenhane and the physician Urban Hiärne, who resisted the great Swedish witch-craze of 1668–77, were both Cartesians.[156] So was Bekker himself in Holland, though his critics insisted that he had muddled the teaching of his master.[157] But the final victory, which liberated Nature from the biblical fundamentalism in which Bekker himself had still been imprisoned, was that of the English deists and the German Pietists,[158] the heirs of the Protestant heretics of the seventeenth century, the parents of that eighteenth-century Enlightenment in which the duel in Nature between a Hebrew God and a medieval Devil was replaced by the benevolent despotism of a modern, scientific 'Deity'.

6

CONCLUSION

I HAVE suggested that the witch-craze of the sixteenth and seventeenth centuries must be seen, if its strength and duration are to be understood, both in its social and in its intellectual context. It cannot properly be seen, as the nineteenth-century liberal historians tended to see it, as a mere 'delusion', detached or detachable from the social and intellectual structure of the time. Had it been so – had it been no more than an artificial intellectual construction by medieval inquisitors – it is inconceiveable that it should have been prolonged for two centuries after its full formulation; that this formulation should never afterwards have been changed; that criticism should have been so limited; that no criticism should have effectively undermined it; that the greatest thinkers of the time should have refrained from openly attacking it; and that some of them, like Bodin, should even have actively supported it. To conclude this essay I shall try to summarize the interpretation I have offered.

First, the witch-craze was created out of a social situation. In its expansive period, in the thirteenth century, the 'feudal' society of Christian Europe came into conflict with social groups which it could not assimilate, and whose defence of their own identity was seen, at first, as 'heresy'. Sometimes it really was heresy: heretical ideas, intellectual in origin, are often assumed by societies determined to assert their independence. So Manichaean ideas, carried – it seems – by Bulgarian missionaries, were embraced by the racially distinct society of Pyrenean France, and 'Vaudois' ideas, excogitated in the cities of Lombardy or the Rhône, were adopted in the Alpine valleys where 'feudal' society could never be established. The medieval Church, as the spiritual organ of 'feudal' society, declared war on these 'heresies', and the friars, who waged that war, defined both orthodoxy and heresy in the process. We know that the doctrines which they ascribed both to the Albigensians and to the Vaudois are not necessarily the doctrines really professed by those 'heretics', whose authentic documents have been almost entirely destroyed by their persecutors. The inquisitors ascribed to the societies which they opposed at once a more elaborate cosmology and a more debased morality than we have any reason to do. In particular, they ascribed to the Albigensians an absolute dualism between God and the Devil in Nature, and orgies of sexual promiscuity – a charge regularly made by the orthodox against esoteric dissenting societies. Both these charges would be carried forward from the first to the second stage of the struggle.

For the first stage was soon over. Orthodox 'feudal' society destroyed the 'Albigensian' and reduced the 'Vaudois' heresies. The friars evangelized the Alpine and Pyrenean valleys. However, the social dissidence remained, and therefore a new rationalization of it seemed necessary. In those mountain areas, where pagan customs lingered and the climate bred nervous disease, the missionaries soon discovered superstitions and hallucinations out of which to fabricate a second set of heresies: heresies less intellectual, and even less edifying, than those which they had stamped out, but nevertheless akin to them. The new 'heresy' of witchcraft, as discovered in the old haunts of the Cathari and the Vaudois, rested on the same dualism of God and the Devil; it was credited with the same secret assemblies, the same promiscuous sexual orgies; and it was described, often, by the same names.

This new 'heresy' which the inquisitors discovered beneath the relics of the old was not devised in isolation. The Albigensians, like their Manichaean predecessors, had professed a dualism of good and evil, God and the Devil, and the Dominicans, the hammers of the Albigensians, like St Augustine, the hammer of the Manichees, had adopted something of the dualism against which they had fought. They saw themselves as worshippers of God, their enemies as worshippers of the Devil; and as the Devil is *simia Dei*, the ape of God, they built up their diabolical system as the necessary counterpart of their divine system. The new Aristotelean cosmology stood firmly behind them both, and St Thomas Aquinas, the guarantor of the one, was the guarantor of the other. The two were interdependent; and they depended not only on each other, but also on a whole philosophy of the world.

The elaboration of the new heresy, as of the new orthodoxy, was the work of the medieval Catholic Church and, in particular, of its most active members, the Dominican friars. No argument can evade or circumvent this fact. The elements of the craze may be non-Christian, even pre-Christian. The practice of spells, the making of weather, the use of sympathetic magic may be universal. The concepts of a pact with the Devil, of night-riding to the sabbat, of *incubi* and *succubi*, may derive from the pagan folk-lore of the Germanic peoples.[159] But the weaving together of these various elements into a systematic demonology which could supply a social stereotype for persecution was exclusively the work, not of Christianity, but of the Catholic Church. The Greek Orthodox Church offers no parallel. There were peasant superstitions in Greece: Thessaly was the classic home of ancient witches. There were encyclopedic minds among the Greek Fathers: no refinement of absurdity deterred a Byzantine theologian. The same objective situation existed in the east as in the west: Manichaean dualism was the heresy of the Bogomils of Bulgaria before it became the heresy of the Albigensians of Languedoc. But even out of the ruins of Bogomilism, the Greek Orthodox Church built up no systematic demonology and launched no witch-craze. By the schism of 1054 the Slavonic countries of Europe – with the exception of Catholic Poland, the exception which proves the rule – escaped participation in one of the most disreputable episodes in Christian history.*

Such, it seems, was the origin of the system. It was perfected in the course of a local struggle and it had, at first, a local application. But the intellectual construction, once complete, was, in itself, universal. It could be applied anywhere. And in the fourteenth century, that century of increasing introversion and intolerance, among the miseries of the Black Death and the Hundred Years War in France, its application was made general. The first of the Avignon popes, themselves bishops from recalcitrant Languedoc, gave a new impulse to the craze. The weapon forged for use against nonconformist societies was taken up to destroy nonconformist individuals: while the inquisitors in the Alps and the Pyrenees continued to multiply the evidence, the warring political factions of France and Burgundy exploited it to destroy their enemies. Every spectacular episode increased the power of the myth. Like the Jew, the witch became the stereotype of the incurable nonconformist; and in the declining Middle Ages, the two were joined as scapegoats for the ills of society. The founding of the Spanish

* This point is made by Riezler, *Geschichte der Hexenprozessen in Baiern*, p. 51, and by Hansen, *Quellen*, p. 71. It may be remarked that the one great Church Father who wrote before the schism and who provided an intellectual basis for the later witch-craze, St Augustine, had little or no influence in Byzantium. This was no doubt partly because he wrote in Latin. Without Augustine, without Aquinas, the Greek Church lacked the cosmological infrastructure of the witch-craze.

Inquisition, which empowered the 'Catholic Kings' to destroy 'judaism' in Spain, and the issue of the Witch Bull, which urged cities and princes to destroy witches in Germany, can be seen as two stages in one campaign.

Even so, the myth might have dissolved in the early sixteenth century. The new prosperity might have removed the need for a social scapegoat. The new ideas of the Renaissance might have destroyed its intellectual basis. We have seen that in the years 1500–1550, outside its Alpine home, the craze died down. In those years the purified Aristoteleanism of Padua corrected the extravagance of scholastic physics; the neo-Platonism of Florence offered a more universal interpretation of Nature; the new criticism of the humanists pared down medieval absurdities. All these intellectual movements might, in themselves, be ambivalent, but they might, together, have been effective. In fact they were not. In the mid sixteenth century, the craze was revived and extended, and the years from 1560 to 1630 saw the worst episodes in its long history. It seems incontestable that the cause of this revival was the intellectual regression of Reformation and Counter-Reformation, and the renewed evangelism of the rival Churches. The former gave new life to the medieval, pseudo-Aristotelean cosmology of which demonology was now an inseparable part. The latter carried into northern Europe the same pattern of forces which the Dominicans had once carried into the Alps and Pyrenees – and evoked a similar response.

The Reformation is sometimes seen as a progressive movement. No doubt it began as such : for it began in humanism. But in the years of struggle, of ideological war, humanism was soon crushed out. The great doctors of the Reformation, as of the Counter-Reformation, and their numerous clerical myrmidons, were essentially conservative : and they conserved far more of the medieval tradition than they would willingly admit. They might reject the Roman supremacy and go back, for their Church system, to the rudimentary organization of the apostolic age. They might pare away the incrustations of doctrine, the monasticism, the 'mechanical devotions', the priestcraft of the 'corrupted' medieval Church. But these were superficial disavowals. Beneath their 'purified' Church discipline and Church doctrine, the Reformers retained the whole philosophic infrastructure of scholastic Catholicism. There was no new Protestant physics, no exclusively Protestant view of Nature. In every field of thought, Calvinism and Lutheranism, like Counter-Reformation Catholicism, marked a retreat, an obstinate defence of fixed positions. And since demonology, as developed by the Dominican inquisitors, was an extension of the pseudo-Aristotelean cosmology, it was defended no less obstinately. Luther might not quote the *Malleus*; Calvin might not own a debt to the Schoolmen; but the debt was clear, and their successors would admit it. Demonology, like the science of which it was a part, was a common inheritance which could not be denied by such conservative Reformers. It lay deeper than the superficial disputes about religious practices and the mediation of the priest.[160]

But if the Reformation was not, intellectually, a progressive movement, it was undoubtedly an evangelical movement. Like the Dominicans of the Middle Ages the Lutheran and Calvinist clergy set out to recover for the faith – for their version of the faith – the peoples of northern Europe whom the Catholic Church had almost lost. In the first generation after Luther this evangelical movement had hardly begun. Luther's appeal was to the Christian princes, to the Christian nobility of Germany. As in the England of Henry VIII, Reform had begun as an affair of state. But by 1560 the princes, or many of them, had been won, and the immediate need was for preachers to establish religion among their people. So the second generation of Reformers, the missionaries formed in Wittenberg or Geneva, poured into the lands of hospitable princes or estates and the Word was preached not only in the ears of the great but in rural parishes in Germany and Scandinavia, France, England and Scotland.

Of course the triumph of the preachers was not always easy. Sometimes they found individual opposition; sometimes whole societies seemed obstinately to refuse their Gospel. Just as the Dominican missionaries had encountered stubborn resistance from the mountain communities of the Alps and Pyrenees, so the Protestant missionaries found their efforts opposed by whole communities in the waste lands of the neglected, half-pagan north. The German preachers found such dissidence in Westphalia, in Mecklenburg, in Pomerania: areas, as a German physician later observed, where the peasants live miserably on thin beer, pig's meat and black bread;[161] the more tolerant Swedish clergy found it, though they did not persecute it, in the racially distinct societies of Lapland and Finland; the Scottish Kirk found it, and persecuted it, among native nonconformists.[162] Sometimes this opposition could be described in doctrinal terms, as 'popery'. 'The Devil, the Mass and witches' were lumped together by John Knox as sustaining the rebellious Countess of Huntly; the Scottish witches who set to sea in a sieve to inconvenience King James were declared to be 'Papists'; and Lancashire, of course, was a nest of both Papists and witches. Sometimes it was too primitive to deserve doctrinal terms, and then a new explanation had to be found. But this time there was no need to invent a new stereotype. The necessary stereotype had already been created by the earlier missionaries and strengthened by long use. The dissidents were witches.

With the Catholic reconquest a generation later, the same pattern repeats itself. The Catholic missionaries too discover obstinate resistance. They too find it social as well as individual. They too find it in particular areas: in Languedoc, in the Vosges and the Jura, in the Rhineland, the German Alps. They too describe it now as Protestant heresy, now as witchcraft. The two terms are sometimes interchangeable, or at least the frontier between them is as vague as that between Albigensians and witches in the past. The Basque witches, says de l'Ancre, have been brought up in the errors of Calvinism. Nothing has spread this pest more effectively through England, Scotland, Flanders and France, declares del Rio (echoing another Jesuit, Maldonado) than *dira Calvinismi lues*. 'Witchcraft grows with heresy, heresy with witchcraft', the English Catholic Thomas Stapleton cried to the sympathetic doctors of Louvain.[163] His argument – his very words – were afterwards repeated, with changed doctrinal labels, by Lutheran pastors in Germany.[164] Whenever the missionaries of one Church are recovering a society from their rivals, 'witchcraft' is discovered beneath the thin surface of 'heresy'.

Such, it seems, is the progress of the witch-craze as a social movement. But it is not only a social movement. From its social basis it also has its individual extension. It can be extended deliberately, in times of political crisis, as a political device, to destroy powerful enemies or dangerous persons. Thus it was used in France in the fourteenth and fifteenth centuries. It can also be extended blindly, in times of panic, by its own momentum. When a 'great fear' takes hold of society, that society looks naturally to the stereotype of the enemy in its midst; and once the witch had become the stereotype, witchcraft would be the universal accusation. It was an accusation which was difficult to rebut in the lands where popular prejudice was aided by judicial torture: we have only to imagine the range of the Popish Plot in England in 1679 if every witness had been tortured. It is in such times of panic that we see the persecution extended from old women, the ordinary victims of village hatred, to educated judges and clergy whose crime is to have resisted the craze. Hence those terrible episodes in Trier and Bamberg and Würzburg. Hence also that despairing cry of the good senator de l'Ancre, that formerly witches were '*hommes vulgaires et idiots, nourris dans les bruyères et la fougière des Landes*', but nowadays witches under torture confess that they have seen at the sabbat '*une infinité de gens de qualité que Satan tient voilez et à couvert pour n'estre cognus*'.[165] It is a sign of such a 'great fear' when the *élite* of society are accused of being in league with its enemies.

Finally, the stereotype, once established, creates, as it were, its own folk-lore, which becomes in itself a centralizing force. If that folk-lore had not already existed, if it had not already been created by social fear out of popular superstition within an intellectually approved cosmology, then psychopathic persons would have attached their sexual hallucinations to other, perhaps more individual figures. This, after all, is what happens today. But once the folk-lore had been created and had been impressed by the clergy upon every mind, it served as a psychological as well as a social stereotype. The Devil with his nightly visits, his *succubi* and *incubi*, his solemn pact which promised new power to gratify social and personal revenge, became 'subjective reality' to hysterical women in a harsh rural world or in artificial communities – in ill-regulated nunneries as at Marseilles, at Loudun, at Louviers, or in special regions like the Pays de Labourd, where (according to de l'Ancre) the fishermen's wives were left deserted for months. And because separate persons attached their illusions to the same imaginary pattern, they made that pattern real to others. By their separate confessions the science of the Schoolmen was empirically confirmed.

Thus on all sides the myth was built up and sustained. There were local differences of course, as well as differences of time; differences of jurisdiction as well as differences of procedure. A strong central government could control the craze while popular liberty often let it run wild. The centralized Inquisition in Spain or Italy, by monopolizing persecution, kept down its production, while north of the Alps the free competition of bishops, abbots and petty lords, each with his own jurisdiction, kept the furnaces at work. The neighbourhood of a great international university, like Basel or Heidelberg, had a salutary effect,* while one fanatical preacher or one over-zealous magistrate in a backward province could infect the whole area. But all these differences merely affected the practice of the moment: the myth itself was universal and constant. Intellectually logical, socially necessary, experimentally proved, it had become a *datum* in European life. Rationalism could not attack it, for rationalism itself, as always, moved only within the intellectual context of the time. Scepticism, the distrust of reason, could provide no substitute. At best, the myth might be contained, as in the early sixteenth century. But it did not evaporate: it remained at the bottom of society, like a stagnant pool, easily flooded, easily stirred. As long as the social and intellectual

---

* The University of Heidelberg deserves particular credit, for it maintained critical standards in a strongly Calvinist country. In 1585, or just before, the faculty of law at Heidelberg opposed the death penalty for witchcraft, saying that it was *'billicher zu Seelsorgern führen dann zur Marten und zum Todte'* – better to cure the soul than to torture and kill the body (cited in Binz, *Doctor Johann Weyer*, pp. 101–2). One of the most powerful opponents of the craze, the Calvinist Hermann Wilchen or Witekind, who wrote under the name 'Lerchheimer von Steinfelden', was professor of mathematics at Heidelberg (see Janssen, *A History of the German People*, XVI, 326). On the other hand the famous Thomas Erastus, professor of medicine, was a firm believer.

structure of which it was a part remained intact, any social fear was likely to flood it, any ideological struggle to stir it, and no piecemeal operation could effectively drain it away. Humanist critics, Paduan scientists, might seek to correct the philosophic base of the myth. Psychologists – medical men like Weyer and Ewich and Webster – might explain away its apparent empirical confirmation. Humane men, like Scot and Spee, by natural reason, might expose the absurdity and denounce the cruelty of the methods by which it was propagated. But to destroy the myth, to drain away the pool, such merely local operations no longer sufficed. The whole intellectual and social structure which contained it, and had solidified around it, had to be broken. And it had to be broken not at the bottom, in the dirty sump where the witch-beliefs had collected and been systematized, but at its centre, whence they were refreshed. In the mid seventeenth century this was done. Then the medieval synthesis, which Reformation and Counter-Reformation had artificially prolonged, was at last broken, and through the cracked crust the filthy pool drained away. Thereafter society might persecute its dissidents as Huguenots* or as Jews. It might discover a new stereotype, the 'Jacobin', the 'Red'. But the stereotype of the witch had gone.

* Thus in 1685 Louis XIV expelled the Huguenots from France as an unassimilable group, but as far as I know, the charges of witch-craft so furiously hurled at the Huguenots of the south in 1609 were not repeated. The Huguenot became again, *per se*, the stereotype of social hatred, and so remained long afterwards, as shown by the Calas affair in 1762. The social significance of that affair is well brought out in David D. Bien, *The Calas Affair: Persecution, Toleration and Heresy in 18th-century Toulouse* (Princeton, 1960).

NOTES

1. Sermon xv, cited in *Materials toward a History of Witchcraft collected by H. C. Lea,* arranged and edited by Arthur C. Howland, with an introduction by George Lincoln Burr (New York, 1957), pp. 178–82; hereafter cited as Lea, *Materials.* (See also p. 21 of the present book.)

2. *Capitulatio de Partibus Saxoniae,* cap. 6. This decree, issued at Paderborn in A.D. 785, is printed in Wilhelm Boudriot, *Die altgermanische Religion (Untersuchungen zur allgemeinen Religionsgeschichte),* ed. Carl Clemen, Heft 2, Bonn, 1928, p. 53.

3. In his *Liber contra insulsam vulgi opinionem de grandine et tonitruis,* written *c.* A.D. 820.

4. Lea, *Materials,* pp. 178–82.

5. Ibid., p. 1252.

6. Ibid., p. 172.

7. *Joannis Filesaci Theologi Parisiensis Opera Varia,* 2nd ed. (Paris, 1614), pp. 703 ff., *'de Idololatria Magica Dissertatio',* Dedication.

8. James VI, *Demonologie, in form of a Dialogue . . .* (Edinburgh, 1597), pp. 66 ff.

9. W. G. Soldan, *Geschichte der Hexenprozesse* (Stuttgart, 1843). Soldan's pioneering work has been twice reprinted, each time with substantial additions and revisions: first by his own son-in-law Heinrich Heppe in 1879; secondly, under the double name of Soldan–Heppe, by Max Bauer in 1911. The differences between the first and the last edition are so great that in this book I shall always distinguish them, citing the original work as Soldan and the later edition as Soldan–Heppe.

10. W. E. H. Lecky, *History of the Rise and Influence of the Spirit of Rationalism in Europe* (1865). My references to this work will be to the edition of 1900.

11. A. D. White, *A History of the Warfare of Science with Theology in Christendom* (New York, 1897).

12. Joseph Hansen, *Quellen und Untersuchungen zur Geschichte des Hexenwahns und der Hexenverfolgung im Mittelalter* (Bonn,

1901); *Zauberwahn, Inquisition und Hexenprozess im Mittelalter* (Munich, 1900); hereafter cited as *Quellen* and *Zauberwahn* respectively.

13. Hansen, *Zauberwahn*, p. 473.

14. Lynn Thorndike, in *Cambridge Medieval History*, VIII, § xxii, 686–7.

15. Jules Michelet, *La Sorcière* (Paris, 1862). My references are to the edition Garnier–Flammarion, 1966.

16. H. C. Lea, *The History of the Inquisition in the Middle Ages* (London and New York, 1888); *The History of the Inquisition in Spain* (New York, 1906).

17. L. Fèbvre, 'Sorcellerie: sottise ou révolution mentale', in *Annales: économies, sociétés, civilisation*, 1948, p. 14.

18. This is the argument of Ludwig Pastor, *History of the Popes*, v, 2nd English ed. (1901), 347.

19. For instances of the use of the term *Vauderye*, see especially Hansen, *Quellen*, pp. 408–15; *Zauberwahn*, pp. 409–18. For *Gazarii*, see *Quellen*, pp. 118, 232.

20. G. L. Burr, 'The Literature of Witchcraft', in *George Lincoln Burr: his Life and Selections from his Writings* (Ithaca, N.Y., 1943), p. 166. This volume will hereafter be cited as Burr, *Life*.

21. Hansen, *Quellen*, p. 18.

22. For Vineti's *Tractatus contra Daemonum Invocatores*, see Lea, *Materials*, p. 272.

23. Julio Caro Baroja, *Las brujas y su mundo*, Madrid, 1961 (English trans. N. Glendinning, *The World of the Witches*, 1964, pp. 103, 143–5).

24. For the history of the *Malleus* and its authors, see Hansen, *Quellen*, pp. 360–407, *Zauberwahn*, pp. 473 ff.

25. '*D'où date la sorcière? Je dis sans hésiter, des temps du désespoir*', Jules Michelet, *La Sorcière*, Introduction.

26. Cf. Hansen, *Zauberwahn*, pp. 400–402; Lea, *Materials*, p. 245.

27. Fernand Braudel, *La Méditerranée et le monde méditerranéen à l'époque de Philippe II* (Paris, 1949), pp. 12–15.

28. Nicolas Eymeric, *Tractatus contra Daemonum Invocatores* (see Lea, *The Inquisition in the Middle Ages*, II, 175).

29. See, for instance, Hansen, *Quellen*, pp. 71, 124, 238–9, 246–51. The Spanish Franciscan Alonso de Espina, in his *Fortalicium Fidei* (Nuremberg, 1494), denounces Jews and witches (whom he calls by their Spanish names) with equal ferocity.

30. Thus at the end of the sixteenth century Juan Maldonado and

Martín del Rio, both Spaniards, taught demonology in France and Flanders respectively, and in the mid seventeenth century we find the Spanish terms, *xurguminae* and *bruxae*, used in a work published in Hungary (J. C. Mediomontanus, *Disputatio Theologica de Lamiis et Veneficis*, Grosswardein, 1656, cited in Lea, *Materials*, p. 1254).

31. Lea, *History of the Inquisition in Spain*, IV, 217–18. For witch-craft cases in Spain outside the Basque provinces, see also Sebastián Cirac Estopañán, *Los procesos de hechicerías en la inquisición de Castilla la Nueva* (Madrid, 1942) and the excellent introduction by Agustín Gonzales de Amezúa to his edition of Cervantes, *El casamiento engañoso y el coloquio de los perros* (Madrid, 1912).

32. Soldan–Heppe, I, 229, 245–6.

33. J. G. Gödelmann, *De Magis, Veneficis et Lamiis . . . Libri III* (Frankfurt, 1591), pp. 51–4.

34. Lea, *Materials*, p. 1253.

35. Pierre de l'Ancre, *L'Incrédulité et mescréance du sortilège pleinement convaincue* (Paris, 1622), pp. 446–501.

36. Lea, *History of the Inquisition in Spain*, IV, 225–39; Jules Michelet, *La Sorcière*, p. 172.

37. See the careful examination by Hansen (summarized in Lea, *Materials*, pp. 337 ff.).

38. Soldan–Heppe, II, I.

39. Lea, *Materials*, p. 1287.

40. See p. 69 of the present book, and note 75.

41. Practically no witches were burnt in Rome in the whole period of the witch-craze. See Nikolaus Paulus, *Hexenwahn und Hexenprozess, vornehmlich im 16ten Jahrhundert* (Freiburg-im-Breisgau, 1910), pp. 260 ff.

42. Is it necessary to document these statements? Then let the reader refer to the works of Américo Castro for the Spanish Inquisition; let him observe the conflict between personal humanity and social fear, in respect of the expulsion of the Moriscos, in the contemporary works of Cervantes and the Spanish *arbitristas*; let him read M. Jean Orcibal's *Louis XIV et les protestants* (Paris, 1951); and let him digest the profound and terrible book of Mr Raul Hilberg, *The Destruction of the European Jews* (Chicago, 1961).

43. Soldan, Lea, and Soldan's twentieth-century editor, Max Bauer, ascribed a great deal of demonological science, but not all, to torture. Lea's disciple and biographer, G. L. Burr, seems, in his essays on witchcraft, to have gone further and to have supposed that torture created witchcraft (cf. *Life*, pp. 177–8).

44. Sir George Mackenzie of Rosehaugh, *The Laws and Customs of Scotland in Matters Criminal* (1678), p. 9.

45. It is gravely mentioned as an *indicium* by Carpzov (cited in Lea, *Materials*, p. 826).

46. Lists of tortures are given in many of the sixteenth- and seventeenth-century manuals – e.g. Benedict Carpzov, *Practica Rerum Criminalium* (1635), quoted in Lea, *Materials*, p. 823. They are also mentioned in reports of trials, eg. Robert Pitcairn, *Criminal Trials in Scotland* (1833), I, pt 2, 215–23. Summaries may be found, for Alsace, in Reuss, *L'Alsace au 17e siècle*; for Lorraine in Ch. Pfister, 'Nicolas Rémy et la sorcellerie en Lorraine à la fin du 16e siècle', in *Revue historique*, 1907; for Germany, in B. Duhr, *Geschichte der Jesuiten in den Ländern deutscher Zunge* (Freiburg-im-Breisgau, 1907–21), II, ii, 482. For the use of *tormentum insomniae* to extract false confessions in our own time see Z. Stypulkowski's account of his own experiences in his book *Invitation to Moscow* (1951).

47. 'Note also', Reginald Scot wrote, 'how easily they may be brought to confess that which they never did, nor lieth in the power of man to do' (*Discovery of Witchcraft*, 1584, epistle to Sir Thomas Scot, J.P.).

48. L. Fèvre, in *Annales: économies, sociétés, civilisations*, 1948, p. 15. By an unfortunate misprint, the word 'Boguet' has here been printed as 'Bossuet', and this error has since been redoubled in an attempt to make it more plausible. In the posthumously published collection of Fèbvre's essays, *Au cœur religieux du XVIe siècle*, the phrase *'un imbécile?'* has been changed into *'Bossuet?'*. No doubt the editor thought that the master had gone too far in describing Bossuet as an imbecile; but in fact it was only the printer who had done so. The 'imbecility' quoted is from Henri Boguet, *Examen des sorciers* (Lyon, 1602), Dedication to the Vicar-General of Besançon.

49. Lea, *Materials*, pp. 1133, 1431–5.

50. Ibid., pp. 1459–61.

51. William Perkins, *A Discourse of the Damned Art of Witchcraft* (Cambridge, 1608), pp. 187–93. The 'patron of witches' whom Perkins is attacking is clearly Reginald Scot. The same point had been made by Bodin.

52. Paolo Grillandi, *Tractatus de Sortilegiis*, 1536 (Lea, *Materials*, pp. 401–5). Jean Bodin, *De la démonomanie des sorciers* (Paris, 1580), Preface.

53. *Procès-verbal fait pour délivrer une fille possédée par le malin esprit à Louviers*, ed. Armand Bénet (Paris, 1883), pp. 38–44, 87–92.

54. See Etienne Delcambre, *Le Concept de la sorcellorie dans le duché de Lorraine au XVIe et XVIIe siècle* (Nancy, 1948–51), fasc. 1, pp. 149–53.

55. Ulricus Molitor, *Tractatus de Pythonicis Mulieribus* (Strasbourg, 1489).

56. Andrea Alciati, *Parergon Juris* (Lea, *Materials*, p. 374); Gianfrancesco Ponzinibio, *Tractatus de Lamiis et Excellentia Juris Utriusque* (ibid., p. 377); Girolamo Cardano, *de Subtilitate* (1550) and *de Rerum Varietate* (1557) (ibid., p. 435); Samuel de' Cassini, *Question de le strie* (1505) (ibid., p. 366).

57. Lynn Thorndike, *History of Magic and Experimental Science*, v (New York, 1941), 110.

58. For Mozzolino, known as Prierlas, see Lea, *Materials*, pp. 354 ff.; for Spina, ibid., pp. 385 ff.; for Dodo, ibid., p. 367. Bodin's attack on Peter of Abano and Alciati is in his *De la démonomanie des sorciers*, Preface.

59. For the leading part played by the Dominicans in the struggle against Luther in Germany, see especially Nikolaus Paulus, *Die deutschen Dominikaner im Kampf gegen Luther 1518–1563* (Freiburg-im-Breisgau, 1903).

60. For the crusade in the Alps and Apennines, see Hansen, *Zauberwahn*, pp. 500–501, *Quellen*, pp. 310–12. The lawyer was Andrea Alciati, who describes his mission in *Parergon Juris*, printed in his *Opera* (Basel, 1558). For the inquisitors in the Spanish Pyrenees, see J. Caro Baroja, *The World of the Witches*, pp. 145–52.

61. For the increase in witch-trials in Germany after the bull, see G. Längin, *Religion und Hexenprozess* (Leipzig, 1888), pp. 76 ff. Bodin implies that witchcraft was of recent introduction in France in his time (Lea, *Materials*, p. 576). Similarly the author of the pamphlet *Les Sorcelleries de Henri de Valoys et les oblations qu'il faisoit au Diable dans le bois de Vincennes* (Paris, 1587) says that France was free from the abominable science of magic in the time of François I and Henri II, and indeed until the time of Henri III and the *Sainte Ligue*.

62. Sigmund Riezler, *Geschichte der Hexenprozessen in Baiern* (Cotta, 1896). Weyer states that, before 1562, the craze had died down in Germany (*de Praestigiis* Daemonum, 1563, Dedication).

63. The *Carolina* was based on the *Constitutio Bambergensis* of 1507, which had been compiled by Johann Freiherr zu Schwarzenberg u. Hohenlandsberg. The article of the *Carolina* on witchcraft

(art. 109) was taken bodily from the *Bambergensis*. The relevant Roman law is the law of Constantine *de Maleficis et Mathematicis*, incorporated in the Code of Justinian.

64. For Zürich, see Paul Schweizer, '*Der Hexenprozess und seine Anwendung in Zürich*', in *Zürcher Taschenbuch*, 1902; Paulus, *Hexenwahn und Hexenprozess*, § VIII, '*Der Hexenwahn bei den Zwinglianern des 16ten Jahrhundert*'. (But Paulus's attempt to prove Zwingli a persecutor *ex silentio* seems to me special pleading.) For Schwyz, see A. Dettling, *Die Hexenprozesse im Kanton Schwyz* (Schwyz, 1907).

65. Paulus, *Hexenwahn und Hexenprozess*, § II, '*Luthers Stellung zur Hexenfrage*', shows the growing credulity of Luther. Luther based his beliefs explicitly on the Bible and old wives' tales, but he was, of course, a renegade friar, and was no doubt familiar with the more systematic demonology of the inquisitors.

66. Paulus, *Hexenwahn und Hexenprozess*, § VIII. The decline of the Zwinglian Church from the liberalism of its founder is further emphasized in the next century. See the account of Bartholomäus Anhorn, *Magiologia* (Basel, 1674), in Lea, *Materials*, p. 747.

67. Paulus, *Hexenwahn und Hexenprozess*, § IV, '*Die Bibel als Autorität für protestantische Hexenverfolgung*', gives many instances of the use of this happy text. For the effect of Calvinism, see G. L. Burr, 'New England's Place in the History of Witchcraft', in *Proceedings of the American Antiquarian Society*, 1911, reprinted in Burr, *Life*, pp. 352–77.

68. The Danish oracle was Niels Hemmingsen (Hemmingius), who published his *Admonitio de Superstitionibus Magicis Vitandis* at Copenhagen in 1575. He had studied at Wittenberg under Luther's successor, Melanchthon, and shows some of the good sense of his master. But he is firm on the subject of the 'good' witch; '*similis est impietas nocere et prodesse arte magica*'; and he explicitly rejects the old distinction of Roman Law. Hemmingius, with his fellow-Lutheran Hyperius, was a main authority of King James, whose interest in demonology, so disastrous to Scotland, seems to have been aroused while he was in Denmark in 1589–90. See Christian Larner, 'Scottish Demonology in the 16th and 17th centuries' (unpublished D.Phil. thesis, Edinburgh University, 1962), pp. 108–10.

69. F. Müller, *Beiträge zur Geschichte des Hexenglaubens und des Hexenprozesses in Siebenburgen* (Brunswick, 1854), pp. 16 ff.

70. For the Jesuits in Germany, see especially Duhr, *Geschichte der Jesuiten in den Ländern deutscher Zunge*, II, ii, 498, etc.; Riezler,

Geschichte der Hexenprozessen in Baiern. The admissions of the Jesuit historian are as telling as any of the accusations of the Protestant. For Franche-Comté, see the documents published by F. Bavoux in *La Sorcellerie en Franche-Comté: Pays de Quingey* (Monaco, 1954) and *Hantises et diableries dans la terre abbatiale de Luxeuil* (Monaco, 1956). See also Lea, *Materials*, pp. 1218–19. For Flanders, see J. B. Cannaert, *Procès des sorcières en Belgique sous Philippe II et le gouvernement des archiducs* (Ghent, 1847). For Poland, see Soldan-Heppe, I, 427.

71. See the controversy on the subject provoked by Adolf Schreiber (Scribonius), *de Examine et Purgatione Sagarum . . . Epistola* (Lemgo, 1583). Schreiber was a physician of Marburg and advocated the test as scientific. His critics included Johann Ewich, state physician of the city of Bremen, and Hermann Neuwaldt, a physician of Brunswick. Ewich described the cold-water test as '*indicium recens repertum sed nunc quoque passim usitatum*' (*De Sagarum . . . Natura, Arte, Viribus et Factis*, Bremen, 1584, sig. D.3); Neuwaldt as a test which he had observed '*nunc denuo vires resumere*' (*Exegesis Purgationis sive Examinis Sagarum*, Helmstedt, 1585). It is mentioned in Weyer's *de Praestigiis Daemonum* (Lea, *Materials*, pp. 524–5). Most lawyers – even Bodin – condemned the cold-water test (see Gödelmann, *de Magis*, I, chap. v. nn. 21, 23, 26–30). But their condemnation was vain: the custom, once adopted, became a new sport with country people, as popular as bear- or bull-baiting. See Francis Hutchinson, *An Historical Essay on Witchcraft* (1718), p. 175. For its use in France, see *Papiers d'état du chancelier Séguier* (Paris, 1964), I, 636–7. I owe this last reference to Mrs Menna Prestwich.

72. *Acts of the Parliament of Scotland*, II, 539.

73. Paulus, *Hexenwahn und Hexenprozess*, pp. 55–7.

74. Thus Melchior Goldast, a Calvinist lawyer and historian, in a memorial submitted to the Catholic Elector of Trier in 1629, declares that witches, whether harmful or not, must be burnt, and gives a list of princes and cities, Catholic, Lutheran and Calvinist, that have adjusted their laws accordingly (*Rechtliches Bedencken von Confiscation der Zauberer- und Hexen-Güther*, Bremen, 1661). See also Lea, *Materials*, p. 805; Paulus, *Hexenwahn und Hexenprozess*, p. 78.

75. 'The singularly favourable contrast which the Anglican Church presents both to continental Catholicism and to Puritanism' is mentioned both by W. E. H. Lecky, *History of the Rise and Influence of . . . Rationalism in Europe*, I, 124–6, and by White, *The Warfare of Science with Theology*, I, 362. Lest religious bias be suspected, it

may be added that White was a Baptist. The same point had been made by Francis Hutchinson, *An Historical Essay on Witchcraft*, Dedication: 'in the main, I believe, our Church of England and its clergy, have as little to answer for, in this respect, as any.' The Erasmian *via media*, the lukewarmth of a non-evangelizing Church, has something to commend it. For Strasbourg, see Lea, *Materials*, pp. 1081, 1208; Reuss, *La Sorcellerie*, pp. 178–81.

76. For the influence of Perkins on the New England Puritans, see Burr, *Life*, p. 366.

77. Perkins, *A Discourse on the Damned Art of Witchcraft*, pp. 173–8, etc.

78. For the witch-law of James I, passed in 1604, see Wallace Notestein, *A History of Witchcraft in England, 1558–1718* (New York, 1909), pp. 101–4.

79. See J. Janssen, *A History of the German People at the Close of the Middle Ages*, trans. by M. A. Mitchell and A. M. Christie (1896–1925), xvi, 307.

80. Notestein, *A History of Witchcraft in England*, p. 116.

81. H. A. Meinders, writing in Lemgo (Westphalia) in 1716, refers to terrible abuses in witch-prosecutions in Westphalia from 1600 to 1700 in which whole towns, especially Herford and Lemgo, have been laid waste (cited in Lea, *Materials*, p. 1432; cf. also the remarks of Jacob Brunnemann, ibid., p. 429). But the persecution had begun well before 1600. It was in Lemgo, in 1583, that Scribonius had published his arguments in favour of the cold-water test, now generally used *'in hisce nostris regionibus, praesertim vero in Westphalia'*. He dedicated his works to the magistrates of Lemgo and Osnabrück whom Ewich and Neuwaldt afterwards accused of 'iniquity and injustice' against witches. The Westphalian jurist Anton Praetorius, who wrote against the craze in 1598–1602, had been driven to protest by the executions he had witnessed there. (See Paulus, *Hexenwahn und Hexenprozess*, § x, *'Der calvinische Prediger Anton Praetorius, ein Bekämpfer der Hexenverfolgung'*). For statistical evidence of the persecution in Osnabrück in the 1580s and 1590s, see Hansen, *Quellen*, p. 545, n. 1.

82. Thus, in the areas ruled by the Protestant, German-speaking city of Bern, the victims came principally from the Catholic, French-speaking Pays de Vaud: see F. Treschsel, *Das Hexenwesen im Kanton Bern* (1870) and H. Vuilleumier, *Histoire de l'Église réformée du Pays de Vaud sous le régime bernois* (Lausanne, 1927–33), ii, 642–721.

83. This is repeatedly stated by de l'Ancre, *L'Incrédulité*.

84. Thus the burden of all Nikolaus Paulus's scholarly essays, printed as *Hexenwahn und Hexenprozess*, is to show (*a*) that before the Reformation all men, including the humanists, believed in witchcraft, so that the Catholic inquisitors deserve no special blame; (*b*) that in the late sixteenth century the Protestants were great burners of witches. Although Paulus carries his interest in Protestant persecution down to the end of the seventeenth century, he shows no interest in the persecutions from 1590 to 1630, which were mainly Catholic.

85. Thus Perkins (*A Discourse on the Damned Art of Witchcraft*) does not mention *succubi* or *incubi* – which are absent also from English witch-trials – and rejects anything which might be regarded as popish 'conjuring'; but he accepts the pact with the Devil and the power of the Devil, by God's permission, to work whatever miracles he likes; from which all else can logically flow, even without the Dominican learning.

86. William V's father, John III, had carried out an Erasmian reform in his duchies, and had secured, as William's tutor, Erasmus's friend Conrad von Heresbach (see A. Wolters, *Conrad von Heresbach*, Elberfeld, 1867). Carl Binz, *Doctor Johann Weyer* ... 2nd ed. (Berlin, 1896), p. 159, describes William V as '*der in den Grundsätzen des Erasmus erzogene Herzog*'. Weyer's own attitude is illustrated by the fact that the whole of his chapter xviii is an extract from Erasmus's *Apologia adversus articulos aliquot per monachos quosdam in Hispaniis exhibitos* (Basel, 1529). Weyer was himself a Protestant, but his Protestantism has to be deduced: it is never stated either by him or his enemies – further evidence of his Erasmian moderation. (See Janssen, *A History of the German People*, xvi, 320–21.) On Weyer see also Leonard Dooren, *Doctor Johannes Wier, Leven en Werken* (Aalten, 1940).

87. This fellow-physician was Johann Ewich, whose letter was printed by Weyer. See above, p. 129, n. 71.

88. Bodin attacked Charles IX as a patron of witches in his *De la démonomanie des sorciers*. Henri III was regularly attacked on the same grounds in the *Ligueur* pamphlets of 1589. See, for instance, *La Vie et faits notables de Henri de Valois*; *L'Athéisme de Henri de Valoys*; *Les Sorcelleries de Henri de Valoys*; *Charmes et caractères de sorcelleries de Henri de Valoys trouvez en la maison de Miron, son premier médecin*. The Erasmianism of the Court of Catherine de Médicis is well brought out by Frances Yates, *The Valois Tapestries* (Studies of the Warburg Institute, 1959), pp. 102–8. For Henri III

as patron of Platonic 'magicians', see Frances Yates, *Giordano Bruno* (1964), p. 180.

89. *Gisberti Voëtii Selectarum Disputationum Theologicarum . . . Pars Tertia* (Utrecht, 1649), pp. 539–632, '*de Magia*'. It is amusing to note this stern Calvinist's deference to public authority: he never mentions Scot without adding '*eius liber titulo* Discoverie of Witch-craft in *Anglia combustus est*', '*fuit tamen liber ille publica auctoritate combustus*', or some such phrase: e.g. pp. 544, 451, 564.

90. It was '*aus habendem Recht und evangelischer Frommigkeit*' that the Protestant Count Ulrich and Count Sebastian von Helfenstein tortured and burnt sixty-three witches in 1562–3 (see Paulus, *Hexenwahn und Hexenprozess*, p. 110).

91. Lea, *Materials*, pp. 1075, 1079, 1232; Soldan, pp. 312–13.

92. *Gesta Trevirorum*, ed. J. H. Wyttenbach and M. F. J. Müller (Trier, 1839), III, 47–57. This fearful account of the persecution in Trier is by a canon of the cathedral who was shocked by its excesses. Parts of it are quoted by Soldan, pp. 358–61; Lea, *Material*, pp. 1188–91; G. L. Burr, *Translations and Reprints from the Original Sources of European History: The Witch Persecutions* (Philadelphia, 1897). The remark about the unique significance of the persecution in Trier is by Burr.

93. For the persecution in Trier, see Lea, *Materials*, pp. 1075, 1189–90; G. L. Burr, 'The Fate of Dietrich Flade', *American Historical Association Papers*, v (1891), 3–57 (partly reprinted in Burr, *Life*, pp. 190–233). For the similar prosperity of the executioner in Schongau, Bavaria, see Riezler, *Geschichte der Hexenprozessen in Baiern*, p. 172. Other instances in Soldan, pp. 314 ff.

94. Franciscus Junius (François du Jon) was French by birth, but naturalized in the Netherlands.

95. Vuilleumier, *Histoire de l'Église réformée*, II, 655–6.

96. Daneau, *de Veneficis . . . Dialogus*, p. 11. Savoy was still one of the main centres of the craze a century later. See P. Bayle, *Réponse aux questions d'un provincial* (Rotterdam, 1704), I, 285.

97. For an account of Rémy, see Ch. Pfister, in *Revue historique*, 1907.

98. P. de l'Ancre, *L'Incrédulité*, Dedication, etc.

99. See *Martini Antonii Delrio e Soc. Jesu . . . Vita brevi commentariolo expressa* (Antwerp, 1609).

100. Montaigne, *Essais*, liv. III, § II.

101. See Götz Freiherr von Pölnitz, *Julius Echter von Mespelbrunn* (Munich, 1934).

102. E.g. Henning Gross (Grosius), *Magica seu mirabilium histori-arum de Spectris* ... *Libri* II (Eisleben, 1597). In his dedication Gross, a Hanoverian bookseller, offers servile gratitude to the prince for his exterminating justice against witches in these days when Satan is more than ever discharging his abominable poison through Christendom.

103. A. Rhamm, *Hexenglaube und Hexenprozesse, vornämlich in den braunschweigischen Landen* (Wolfenbüttel, 1882). Cf. Soldan–Heppe, 11, 59 ff.

104. The manuscript was discovered in 1886 by G. L. Burr. See his account published in *The Nation* (New York), 11 November 1886.

105. For King James's conversion, see Notestein, *A History of Witchcraft in England*, pp. 137–45.

106. Duhr, *Geschichte der Jesuiten*, 11, ii, 498. The point had already been made, in an indirect way, by the witch-burning Bishop Forner of Bamberg, when he inquired, in his *Panoplia Armaturae Dei* (see note 111), why it was that there were so many witches in Catholic lands and so few in Protestant. And cf. Soldan–Heppe, 1, 426–7.

107. See Friedrich Merzbacher, *Die Hexenprozesse in Franken* (Munich, 1957).

108. Lea, *Materials*, pp. 1203–4.

109. This was reported by a correspondent of Count Werner von Salm. The document is quoted in W. v. Waldbrühl, *Naturforschung und Hexenglaube* (Berlin, 1867).

110. See Bavoux, *Hantises et diableries dans la terre abbatiale de Luxeuil*, pp. 128–9.

111. *Panoplia Armaturae Dei adversus* ... *Magorum et Sagarum Infestationes* (1625).

112. For the persecution in Bamberg, see Johann Looshorn, *Geschichte des Bisthums Bamberg* (Munich, 1886), v, 55; Merzbacher, *Die Hexenprozesse in Franken*, pp. 42 ff.

113. Other protests include Theodor Thumm, *Tractatus Theologicus de sagarum impietate* ... (Tübingen, 1621); the anonymous *Malleus Judicum*, of about 1626 (Lea, *Materials*, p. 690; but see also Paulus, *Hexenwahn und Hexenprozess*, pp. 193–4); Justus Oldekop, *Cautelarum Criminalium Sylloge* (Brunswick, 1633), on which see Burr's note in Lea, *Materials*, p. 850.

114. According to Leibniz, Philipp von Schönborn '*fit cesser ces brûleries aussitôt qu'il parvint à la Régence; en quoi il a été suivi par les ducs de Brunswic et enfin par la plupart des autres princes et états d'Allemagne*' (*Théodicée*, 1, 144–5, § 97).

115. Paulus, *Hexenwahn und Hexenprozess*, § VI; Ernst Boll, *Mecklenburgische Geschichte . . . neu bearbeitet von Dr Hans Witte*, II (Wismar, 1913), pp. 123 ff.

116. '*Nulla est fere hodie frequentior disputatio quam quae de sortilegiis et divinationibus suscipitur.*' For Pcña, see Hansen, *Quellen*, pp. 357–9. He concluded that *incubi* and *succubi* were real and that the night-flight to the sabbat was proved beyond doubt.

117. C. L. Ewen, *Witch Hunting and Witch Trials* (1924), p. 113.

118. The Lapland witches were first reported in Olaus Magnus, *de Gentibus Septentrionalibus* (Rome, 1555), pp. 119–28; thereafter they became famous in Europe. Cf. Milton, *Paradise Lost*, II, 665.

119. Bertil Sundborg, '*Gustaf Rosenhane och Trolldomsväsendet*', in *Lychnos* (Uppsala, 1954–5), pp. 203–64. I am indebted to Professor Michael Roberts for his help in interpreting the Swedish evidence.

120. Thus Weyer states that witches were not burnt in the dominions of the Duke of Cleves, and he names several other princes who were equally firm and equally effective, e.g. the Elector Frederick of the Palatinate and Duke Adolf of Nassau. The princes of Hesse, Philip the Magnanimous and William V, the Wise, similarly controlled the persecution in their lands. Cf. the effect of James I's conversion in England. On the other hand the extension of the persecution when princes gave free rein, or positively encouraged it, is obvious: perhaps nowhere so obvious as in the prince-bishoprics of Germany.

121. Thus, while Weyer relied on the Duke of Cleves and Weyer's supporters Johann Ewich and Hermann Neuwaldt on Count Simon of Lippe-Redtburg and (vain hope!) Heinrich Julius of Brunswick-Lüneburg, their critic Schreiber dedicated his works to the magistrates of Lemgo and of Osnabrück '*dominis suis et fautoribus optimis*'. In general, local magistrates remained the guarantors of the craze, while the best hope of reformers was to secure the support of a prince. Cf. the statements of the magistrates of Dôle, in Franche-Comté, (p. 84 of this book) and the protests of the parlement of Rouen against Colbert's order prohibiting witch-trials (*Lecky, History of the Rise and Influence of . . . Rationalism in Europe*, I, 98–9). In Mecklenburg – as in Scotland – the triumph of the witch-burners coincided with the triumph of the Estates over the prince. The Swedish outbreak of 1667 took place while the power of the Crown was in abeyance.

122. See Lucien Fèbvre, in *Annales: économies, sociétés, civilisations*, 1948, p. 15.

123. Francis Osborne, *Advice to his Son* [1656], ed. E. A. Parry (1896), p. 125. Among books against witch-trials at that time are Sir Robert Filmer, *An Advertisement to the Jury-men of England touching Witches* (1653); Thomas Ady, *A Candle in the Dark* (1656).

124. Lea, *Materials*, pp. 743–4; Burr, *Life*, p. 186. For the effect of the Roman *instructio* in Poland, see Lea, *Materials*, pp. 1232, 1273.

125. Riezler, *Geschichte der Hexenprozessen in Baiern*, p. 282.

126. Reuss, *L'Alsace au 17e siècle*, II, 105.

127. P. de Félice, *Lambert Daneau, sa vie, ses ouvrages, ses lettres inédites* (Paris, 1882).

128. Both Junius and Rivetus expressed their views in commentaries on Exodus xxii 18: Franciscus Junius, *Libri Exodi Analytica Explicatio* (Leiden, 1598); Andreas Rivetus, *Commentarius in Exodum* (Leiden, 1634). Junius also translated Bodin's *Démonomanie*

129. *Gisberti Voëtii Selectarum Disputationum Theologicarum* . . . *Pars Tertia*, pp. 539–632, '*de Magia*'. Voëtius, who dominated Utrecht till his death in 1678, at the age of eighty-seven, first wrote this work in 1636 and amplified it in later editions. His arguments were repeated with approval by Johann Christian Frommann, *Tractatus de Fascinatione Novus et Singularis* (Nuremberg, 1675). The spirit of Voëtius lingered long in Utrecht. In 1709 a preacher of Utrecht, Jacob de la Faye, defended the reality of witchcraft against the subversive arguments of the English deist, John Toland. See Jacobus Fayus, *Defensio Religionis* . . . (Utrecht, 1709).

130. See Johann Greve [Graevius], *Tribunal Reformatum* (Hamburg, 1624). Greve was influenced by Weyer whom he often quotes. See Binz, *Doctor Johann Weyer*.

131. J. A. van Dorsten, *Thomas Basson, 1555–1613, English Printer at Leiden* (Leiden, Sir Thomas Browne Institute, 1961), pp. 49–54.

132. Jacobus Scheltema, *Geschiedenis der Heksenprocesen* (Haarlem, 1828), p. 258. Dr R. B. Evenhuis, *Ook dat was Amsterdam: de Kerk der her hervorming in de gouden eeuw* (Amsterdam, 1965–7), II, 127–8, shows that the last witch-burning in Amsterdam took place shortly before 1578; but his statement that this ended such burnings in the (United) Netherlands is refuted by the factual evidence given by Scheltema; and in describing the cessation as 'the glory of the Amsterdam magistrates *and Church Council*' [my italics], he seems to me to claim too much for the Church of which he is a minister.

133. See, for instance, the enlightened letter sent by Léonor d'Estampes de Valençay, Archbishop and Duke of Reims, to the chancellor, Séguier, on 28 July 1644, quoted in *Lettres et mémoires*

du chancelier Séguier, ed. Roland Mousnier (Paris, 1964), 1, 636–7.

134. '*Cum inter ruentis seculi calamitates, quas (proh dolor!) non tam legimus quam passim experimur . . . mundi vespere ad occasum declinante et malicia hominum excrescente . . .*' etc. etc. *Malleus Maleficarum* (Apologia).

135. This important discovery was made by Francis Potter, a versatile scientist, on 10 December 1625. Though announced from royalist Oxford, it was hailed with ecstasy in Puritan Cambridge, and in a work published by order of the Long Parliament and introduced by the Prolocutor of the Westminster Assembly it was advertised as 'the greatest mystery that hath ever been discovered since the beginning of the world'. See Francis Potter, *An Interpretation of the Number of the Beast* (Oxford, 1642); Joseph Mede, *The Key of the Revelation searched and demonstrated* (1643), Preface by William Twisse; *The Works of Joseph Mede B.D.*, ed. John Worthington (1664), pp. 1036, 1044, 1076; John Aubrey, *Brief Lives*, 'Francis and Hannibal Potter'.

136. Jacob Brunnemann, *Discours von betrüglichen Kennzeichen der Zauberey* (Stargard, 1708), cited in Lea, *Materials*, p. 1427.

137. This point was made by Soldan in 1843 and has been repeated ever since.

138. A. van der Linde, *Balthasar Bekker Bibliographie* (The Hague, 1869), lists 134 contemporary works concerning Bekker. Apart from one in French (see next note) and two in Latin, all are in Dutch.

139. Benjamin Binet, *Traité historique des dieux et des démons* (Delft, 1696). The English translation of Bekker's work appeared under the title *The World turn'd upside down . . .* (1700).

140. John Beaumont, *An Historical, Physiological and Theological Treatise of Spirits* (1705). This work is not mentioned by van der Linde.

141. Eberhard David Hauber, *Bibliotheca Acta et Scripta Magica* (Lemgo, 1739), 1, 565. Hauber was a liberal Lutheran clergyman whose work – reprints of earlier texts illustrating the witch-craze – helped to liberalize the public opinion of Germany. But, like Thomasius, he was critical of Bekker.

142. A German translation of Wagstaffe's *Question of Witchcraft Debated* (1669) was published at Halle, dedicated to Thomasius, in 1711. Thomasius himself wrote a preface to a German translation of Webster's *The Displaying of Supposed Witchcraft*, which was also published at Halle in 1719.

143. How little Bekker had to do with the destruction of belief among the Dutch laity is shown by the remarks of a French officer

Notes

who visited Holland with the Prince de Condé in 1673 – nearly twenty years before Bekker wrote. He reported that at that time most Dutchmen regarded Hell as a 'phantom' and Paradise as 'an agreeable chimera' invented by the clergy to encourage virtue. See G.-B. Stoppa, *La Religion des Hollandois* ... (Paris, 1673), p. 88.

144. Burr, *Translations and Reprints*, p. 1.

145. Lea, *Materials*, pp. 494–6, 511, etc.

146. The passage is in Macaulay's essay on Ranke's *History of the Popes*.

147. Vitoria was the greatest of the philosophers of Salamanca: see Marjorie Grice-Hutchinson, *The School of Salamanca* (Oxford, 1952). He dealt with witchcraft in his *Relectiones XII Theologicae* (relectio x, '*de Arte Magica*'), written about 1540 and first published at Lyon in 1557.

148. For the roving humanist life of Hyperius (i.e. Andreas Gerhard of Ypres) see Wigandus Orthius, *Oratio de vita ac obitu ... Andreae Hyperii* (Marburg, 1564). He wrote on education, historiography, rhetoric, arithmetic, geometry, cosmography, optics, astronomy, and all branches of divinity. He also commented on Aristotle's Physics and Ethics. His demonology is set out in *Andreae Hyperii Methodi Theologici* ... (Basel, 1567). This – or the praise of King James – caused him to be described, with Hemmingius, unfairly, as a 'popish bloodsucker' by Thomas Ady, *A Candle in the Dark* (1656).

149. H. Nicolai, *de Cognitione Humana Universa, hoc est de omni scibili humano* (Danzig, 1648); *de Magicis Actionibus* (Danzig, 1649). Nicolai was a 'syncretist', and therefore relatively liberal.

150. Thorndike, *History of Magic and Experimental Science*, v, 69.

151. P. de l'Ancre (*Tableau de l'inconstance des mauvais anges et démons*, Paris, 1613, p. 77) remarks that '*le cœur et l'âme du sieur de Montaigne*' was the fashionable Jesuit Maldonado, who used scepticism only in the cause of orthodoxy. Maldonado preached against witches in Paris and was the acknowledged teacher (*meus quondam doctor*) of del Rio. See Martín del Rio, *Disquisitionum Magicarum Libri VI* (Louvain, 1599–1600) '*Proloquium*', and 1, 210; J. Maldonado, '*Praefatio de Daemonibus et eorum praestigiis*', printed in H. M. Prat, '*Maldonat et l'Université de Paris*' (Paris, 1856), pp. 567 ff.; Clément Sclafert, '*Montaigne et Maldonat*', *Bulletin de Littérature Ecclésiastique* LII (Toulouse, 1951), pp. 65–93, 129–46.

152. P. Bayle, *Réponse aux questions d'un provincial*, chs. xxxv–xliv; J. Glanville, *Some Philosophical Considerations touching the being of witches* (1666); etc.

153. Bacon's few observations on witches, noncommittal in general, incredulous in particular, are cited in Lea, *Materials*, p. 1355. For his positive views on 'magic', see P. Rossi, *Francesco Bacone, dalla magia alla scienza* (Bari, 1951). Selden has been credited with reactionary beliefs on account of one lawyerly observation in his *Table-Talk*, which in fact indicates scepticism, not belief: his real 'Platonic' views on Nature can be seen in his *de Diis Syris* (1617), syntagma 1, cap. 2. Grotius not only believed generally in a universal order of Nature: specifically he rejected the penalties of the Mosaic law, which were the basis of witch-persecution in Protestant countries (*de Jure Belli ac Pacis*, lib. 1, cap. 1, xvi, '*Jure Hebraeorum numquam obligatos fuisse alienigenas*'); repudiated biblical fundamentalism (much to the indignation of good Calvinists); and in his Annotations on the Old and New Testaments followed the example of Erasmus in omitting to comment on the passages customarily cited in support of witch-beliefs.

154. Lea's lack of sympathy with any rationalism but his own is shown by his remarks on Erastus and Paracelsus. Erastus, he says, 'was superior to many of the superstitions of the age, as is shown in his criticism of Paracelsus, and yet a believer in witchcraft' (*Materials*, p. 430). It evidently did not occur to Lea that the rationalism of Erastus entailed belief in witchcraft, while the 'superstition' of Paracelsus might create the context of a new rationalism which would dispense with it.

155. Thomasius, *de Crimine Magiae* (Halle, 1701, § XLVII). Cf. F. M. Brahm, *Disputatio Inauguralis* ... (1701), in Lea, *Materials*, p. 1406.

156. Bertil Sundborg, in *Lychnos*, 1954–5, pp. 204–64.

157. Even the sympathetic Hauber made this criticism (*Bibliotheca ... Magica*, 1, 565).

158. It is perhaps unfair to isolate Thomasius from the other Pietists, just as it would be unfair to isolate Bekker from other Cartesians. The founder of the Pietist movement, P. J. Spener, had preceded Thomasius in opposing witch-beliefs in his *Theologische Bedencken* (1700); Gottfried Arnold, who defended the heretics of the past in his *Unparteyische Kirche- und Ketzerhistorie* (1699), co-operated with Thomasius; and it was from the university press of Halle, the centre of Pietism, that nearly all the German books against the witch-craze were sent forth.

159. This is stated by Weiser-Aall in Bächtold-Stäubli, *Handwörterbuch des deutschen Aberglauben III* (Berlin and Leipzig, 1930–31), pp. 1828 ff., s.v. '*Hexe*'.

160. Paulus (*Hexenwahn und Hexenprozess*, § iv), in his attempts to spare the medieval Catholic Church, argues that the Protestant Reformers derived their demonology not from their Catholic predecessors but direct from Germanic mythology. This argument (which is also used by the Catholic apologist Janssen) depends, once again, on an improper isolation of witch-beliefs from general cosmology. If Luther had rejected the Aristotelean cosmology while accepting witch-beliefs, then it *might* be said that he derived those beliefs from pagan sources – although even then the argument would be very strained. But since he, like Calvin, accepted the basic cosmology of the medieval Church, there is no need for such ingenuity. When the front door is wide open, why make a detour in search of a back passage?

161. Friedrich Hoffmann, *Dissertatio Physico-Medica de Diaboli Potentia in Corporu* (Halle, 1703), quoted in Lea, *Materials*, p. 1466; and see Lea's note, ad loc. Cf. also Brunnemann, *Discours von betrüglichen Kennzeichen der Zauberey*, cited in Lea, *Materials*, p. 1429, which also gives Westphalia, Pomerania and Mecklenburg as the homes of witches.

162. In the first edition of this essay I here wrote that the Kirk found its earliest victims 'among the Celtic Highlanders'. I am now satisfied that this is wrong. In Celtic Scotland, as in Celtic Ireland, the established Protestant Church found few witches – perhaps because it did not look for them: before the eighteenth century it made little effort to penetrate or evangelize those 'barbarous' tribal areas.

163. 'Crescit cum magia haeresis, cum haeresi magia.' Thomas Stapleton's dissertation on the question 'Cur magia pariter cum haeresi hodie creverit', delivered on 30 August 1594, is printed in *Thomae Stapleton Angli S.T.D. Opera Omnia* (Paris, 1620), II, 502–7.

164. Hauber (*Bibliotheca ... Magica*, II, 205) states that he possessed a copy of Stapleton's dissertation as emended for delivery in a Lutheran university during the great witch-craze of the late 1620s. The words 'Luther' and 'Lutherans' had been changed into 'the Pope' and 'the Jesuits'; otherwise no alteration had been thought necessary: a nice commentary on the intellectual originality of both sides. The good Lutheran had left Stapleton's abuse of the Calvinists intact.

165. P. de l'Ancre, *Tableau de l'inconstance des mauvais anges et démons* (Paris, 1613), Dedication to Mgr de Sillery, chancelier de France.

INDEX

Abano, Peter of, medieval physician, 58, 61

Agobard, St, Bishop of Lyon, 13

Agrippa, Henry Cornelius, 57, 59, 61, 73, 108

Alba, Pedro de Toledo, 4th Duke of, 74

Albigensians, their connexion with witchcraft, 25–7, 40, 43, 52, 70–71, 104, 113–14

Alciati, Andrea, 57, 61, 127

Alexander IV, Pope, 26

Alexander VI, Pope, 33

Alsace: witch-craze in, 29, 98; diabolical peculiarity in, 17n

Amadeus VIII, Duke of Savoy (Pope Felix V), 'eldest son of Satan', 27

Anabaptism, German, 70

Ancre, Pierre de l', an enchanting persecutor, 36, 57n, 67, 79, 86, 100, 108, 119, 120, 137

Anglican Church, sound on witches, 129–30

Anti-semitism, compared with witch-hunting, 22

Apocalypse, its dubious authorship, 56

Aquinas, St Thomas: his magisterial ruling on *incubi*, 17–18; advantages of ignoring him, 115n; mentioned, 106, 114

Aristoteleanism: compatible with demonology, 48, 114; except in Padua, 58, 62, 116

Arminius, Jacobus, opposed to witch-beliefs, 99

Arnold, Gottfried, German Pietist, 138

Augustine of Hippo, St: a father of the witch-craze, 13, 17; a hammer of the Manichees, 53n, 114, 115n

Bacon, Francis, Lord Verulam, Viscount St Albans, reserved on witches, 57n, 109–10

Basson, Thomas, English Arminian printer at Leiden, 99

Bavaria: disgusting orthodoxy of, 71n; witch-craze in, 66; killed by a Theatine monk, 48

Baxter, Richard, 97

Bayle, Pierre, on witchcraft, 108, 132

Beast, the fugitive number of, discovered by Rev. Francis Potter, F.R.S., 101, 136

Bedford, Jacquette, Duchess of, tried as a witch, 1470, 54

Bekker, Balthasar, Cartesian Dutch minister, 101–3, 109, 111

Belzebuh, a big black man, 50

Benedict XII, Pope, 26

Bernard of Como, inquisitor, 27

Bernardino of Siena, an anti-semitic saint, 33

Bérulle, Pierre de, cardinal, 12

Beza, Theodore, 98

Binet, Benjamin, 102, 136

Binsfield, Peter, suffragan Bishop of Trier, a witch-burner, 67, 72, 77–8, 82, 158

Bodin, Jean, the Aristotle of the sixteenth century, 45, 47, 49, 50, 61, 74, 78, 86, 100, 107, 113

Bogomils, Bulgarian heretics, 112, 115

Boguet, Henri, witch-doctor, 47, 77–8, 80, 100, 106

Boniface, St, disbelieves in witches, 13

Bossuet, Jacques-Bénigne, Bishop of Meaux, inadvertently maligned by French printer, 126

Braudel, Fernand, 30

Browne, Sir Thomas, 97

Bruno, Giordano, 59, 62, 80

Bucer, Martin, keeps Strasbourg sane, 69

Burr, George Lincoln, 104, 125

Byzantium, no witch-craze in, 114

Calvin, John: his view on witches, 64–5; his debt to the Schoolmen, 117; mentioned, 68, 98

Calvinism, and the witch-craze, 64–119 *passim*

Campanella, Tomaso, 62

Canisius, St Peter, S.J., 66

Cardano, Girolamo, 57, 59, 62, 108

Carpocrates, second-century heresiarch, 52n

Carpzov, Benedict, Lutheran witch-lawyer, 72, 86, 100, 126

Cartesianism: alarms Swedish Church, 92; undermines witch-beliefs, 110–11. *See also* Descartes